Best Ever Curries and Casseroles

CONTENTS

EDITORIAL
Food Editor Sheryle Eastwood
Assistant Food Editor Rachel Blackmore
Home Economist Anneka Mitchell
Recipe Development Michelle Gorry, Carolyn Fienberg,
Voula Mantzouridis
Food Consultant Frances Naldrett
Text Alison Magney
Editorial Co-ordinator Margaret Kelly
Editor Marian Broderick

PHOTOGRAPHY
Yanto Noerianto

STYLING
Jacqui Hing
Rosemary De Santis

ILLUSTRATIONS
Carol Dunn

DESIGN AND PRODUCTION
Tracey Burt
Chris Hatcher

PUBLISHER
Philippa Sandall

Published by J.B. Fairfax Press Pty Ltd
80-82 McLachlan Avenue
Rushcutters Bay 2011
©J.B.Fairfax Press Pty Ltd, 1990

ISBN 1 86343 057 1
Includes Index

Formatted by J.B. Fairfax Press Pty Ltd
Output by Savage Type, Brisbane
Printed by Toppan Printing Co, Hong Kong

Distributed Internationally by
T.B. Clarke (Overseas) Pty Ltd
80 McLachlan Avenue
Rushcutters Bay NSW 2011
Ph: (0933) 402330 Fax: (0933) 402234

Distributed by J.B. Fairfax Press Ltd
9 Trinity Centre, Park Farm Estate
Wellingborough, Northants
Ph: (0933) 402330 Fax: (0933) 402234

Distributed in Australia by
Newsagents Direct Distributors
150 Bourke Road, Alexandria NSW
Supermarket distribution
Storewide Magazine Distributors
150 Bourke Road, Alexandria NSW

CHECK-AND-GO

When planning a meal, use the easy
Check-and Go boxes which appear
beside each ingredient. Simply check
on your pantry shelf and if the
ingredients are not there, tick the
boxes as a reminder to add those
items to your shopping list.

INTRODUCTION

Some of the most delicious concoctions to come out of any kitchen are in those quiet, lidded pots which simmer away slowly on the back burner, or are hidden away in a slow oven, taking in more flavour with every passing minute. Of the nearly 100 recipes tried, tasted (OK, devoured) and presented in this book, there will be dozens you'll reach for again and again.

We have some fiery suggestions for those who love a really good assault on the tastebuds. For those who like a hint of spice without the heat, there are recipes featuring evocative herbs and spices.

For the 'teenagers' of the tastebuds, those who like milder dishes, we have some low-key satays, kebabs, vegetable dumplings and a whole lot more.

There's no need to sacrifice taste, as we'll show you, even though in every family, someone is always watching their weight, cholesterol, fat intake, fibre content and/or salt consumption - and some just prefer to eat lightly most of the time. Our luscious ingredients taste so good that you'd think they should be bad for you, almost by rights!

Lastly, we look at the hearty meals all families love to devour, every now and again, but with new twists onto some old faithfuls that'll completely surprise you.

This book will inspire you to get out your deepest pots, reorganise your spices, grow your own fresh herbs and eagerly get back into tasty, satisfying cooking again.

Hot Dishes

*Hold on to your tastebuds!
They're about to be
stimulated by lime juice,
fresh ginger, fiery chillies,
robust mustards and
aggressive spices. Those of
you who think nothing beats
tucking into a dish that
makes your eyes water will
be delighted with this
selection of recipes.*

*Tandoori Lamb Cutlets,
Pungent Spinach Curry*

TANDOORI LAMB CUTLETS

Tandoori is a favourite Indian way of cooking. Traditionally the food is cooked in a vat shaped clay oven called a Tandoor. In our recipe we have used the traditional spices and flavourings of the tandoori and then we grill our cutlets.

Serves 4

☐ **8 lamb cutlets**

MARINADE
☐ **4 tablespoons unflavoured yoghurt**
☐ **1 teaspoon grated fresh ginger**
☐ **1 clove garlic, crushed**
☐ **1 tablespoon lime juice**
☐ **1 teaspoon ground cumin**
☐ **$1/4$ teaspoon ground cardamom**
☐ **$1/4$ teaspoon chilli powder**
☐ **$1/4$ teaspoon garam masala**
☐ **few drops red food colouring**

1   Trim meat of all visible fat and set aside.
2   To make marinade, combine yoghurt, ginger, garlic, lime juice, cumin, cardamom, chilli powder and garam masala. Add red food colouring until the marinade is pink. Add cutlets, toss to coat and set aside to marinate for 30 minutes.
3   Remove cutlets from marinade. Grill or barbecue for 6–8 minutes, turning and basting with marinade frequently.

❖

PUNGENT SPINACH CURRY

Our quick spinach curry makes a wonderful dish for a vegetarian meal or for use as an accompaniment to a mild meat dish.

Serves 6

☐ **60 g (2 oz) ghee**
☐ **1 onion, finely chopped**
☐ **2 cloves garlic, crushed**
☐ **2 small red chillies, finely sliced**
☐ **1 teaspoon grated fresh ginger**
☐ **500 g (1 lb) fresh spinach, stalks removed and leaves shredded**

1   Melt ghee in a frypan, cook onion, garlic, chillies, and ginger for 2–3 minutes or until onion softens.
2   Add spinach leaves and toss to coat with spices. Cook for 4–5 minutes or until spinach begins to wilt. Season to taste with salt and pepper.

CHICK PEA FRITTERS

Chick peas, with their distinctive crunchy texture and nutty flavour, are popular throughout the Middle East and India. In this recipe we turn them into delicious fritters, ideal for a vegetarian meal. Serve our spicy fritters with a fresh tomato sauce.

Makes 25

- ☐ **250 g (8 oz) chick peas**
- ☐ **1 onion, chopped**
- ☐ **2 cloves garlic, crushed**
- ☐ **30 g (1 oz) chopped fresh parsley**
- ☐ **2 small red chillies, finely chopped**
- ☐ **1 tablespoon chopped fresh coriander**
- ☐ **$^1/_2$ teaspoon ground cumin**
- ☐ **freshly ground black pepper**
- ☐ **2 eggs**
- ☐ **3 tablespoons plain flour**
- ☐ **2 teaspoons baking powder**
- ☐ **oil for cooking**

1   Place chick peas in a large glass bowl, cover with water and soak for 48 hours. Change water daily.

2   Drain chick peas and place in a food processor or blender with onion, garlic, parsley, chillies, coriander, cumin, pepper and eggs. Transfer to a mixing bowl and fold through flour and baking powder.

3   Heat oil in a frypan, cook heaped tablespoonfuls of mixture until golden brown. Remove from pan with a slotted spoon and drain on absorbent paper.

Above: Chick Pea Fritters,
Red Hot Kidney Beans
Right: Fish Cutlets with Hot Peanut Sauce

FRESH TOMATO SAUCE

Fresh tomato sauces are great to serve with vegetables, chicken, fish or grilled meats. You may prefer to replace the basil with a mixture of fresh herbs. Dried herbs can be used if necessary.

Makes 500 mL (1 pt)

- ☐ **2 tablespoons olive oil**
- ☐ **1 large onion, chopped**
- ☐ **1 clove garlic, crushed**
- ☐ **440 g (14 oz) canned tomatoes, undrained and mashed**
- ☐ **125 mL (4 fl.oz) dry white wine**
- ☐ **2 tablespoons chopped fresh basil**
- ☐ **freshly ground black pepper**

1   Heat oil in a saucepan. Cook onion and garlic for 4–5 minutes or until onion softens. Stir in tomatoes and wine and simmer for 5 minutes.

2   Add 1 tablespoon basil and simmer for a further 1 hour or until sauce thickens and reduces. Just before serving, stir in remaining basil and season to taste with pepper.

RED HOT KIDNEY BEANS

With such a delicious combination of flavours, our red hot beans will be a favourite with all those who love chilli.

Serves 6

- ☐ **185 g (6 oz) red kidney beans, washed and drained**
- ☐ **1.2 L (2 pts) water**
- ☐ **3 tablespoons ghee**
- ☐ **1 onion, chopped**
- ☐ **$^1/_4$ teaspoon ground cumin**
- ☐ **1 clove garlic, crushed**
- ☐ **2 red chillies, finely chopped**
- ☐ **1 teaspoon grated fresh ginger**
- ☐ **1 tablespoon lime juice**
- ☐ **$^1/_4$ teaspoon garam masala**
- ☐ **125 mL (4 fl. oz) light sour cream**

1 Place beans in a large saucepan, cover with water and bring to the boil. Reduce heat and simmer for 2 minutes. Remove pan from heat and stand beans, uncovered, for 1 hour.

2 Return beans to the boil, boil for 10 minutes. Reduce heat, cover and simmer for 1 hour. Place half the beans and liquid in a food processor or blender. Process until smooth and return to the pan.

3 Heat ghee in a large frypan, cook onion for 2–3 minutes or until golden. Stir in cumin, garlic, chillies and ginger and cook for 1 minute. Add beans to pan, cook gently for 1–2 minutes.

4 Combine lime juice, garam masala and sour cream. Stir into bean mixture, and heat through gently.

FISH CUTLETS WITH HOT PEANUT SAUCE

Serves 4

- ☐ **2 tablespoons ghee**
- ☐ **4 white fish cutlets**

PEANUT SAUCE
- ☐ **110 g (3$^1/_2$ oz) roasted unsalted peanuts, finely chopped**
- ☐ **2 teaspoons sambal oelek**
- ☐ **$^1/_2$ teaspoon chilli powder**
- ☐ **1 tablespoon brown sugar**
- ☐ **1 tablespoon soy sauce**
- ☐ **185 mL (6 fl.oz) coconut milk**
- ☐ **1 teaspoon grated lemon rind**
- ☐ **2 teaspoons lemon juice**

1 Heat ghee in a frypan, cook cutlets for 3–4 minutes each side or until fish flakes when tested with a fork.

2 To make peanut sauce, combine peanuts, sambal oelek, chilli powder, sugar, soy sauce, coconut milk, lemon rind and lemon juice in a saucepan. Cook over medium heat, without boiling, until heated through. Spoon sauce over fish and serve.

BUYING FRESH FISH

✧ When buying fish fillets they should be shiny and firm with a pleasant sea smell.

✧ Whole fish should have a pleasant sea smell and a bright lustre to the skin. Gills should be red and the eyes bright and bulging. When touched, the flesh should be firm and springy.

✧ Fillets that are dull, soft, discoloured or 'ooze' water when touched indicate fish that is past its best.

✧ Dull-coloured fish with sunken eyes should be avoided at all costs.

CHICKEN BIRYANI

The great Mogul emperors served biryani at lavish feasts on plates so large that two people were required to carry them.

Serves 4

- ☐ **3 tablespoons ghee**
- ☐ **3 onions, sliced**
- ☐ **1.5 kg (3 lb) chicken pieces**
- ☐ **2 teaspoons grated fresh ginger**
- ☐ **3 cloves garlic, crushed**
- ☐ **¹/₂ teaspoon ground cumin**
- ☐ **¹/₂ teaspoon ground cinnamon**
- ☐ **¹/₄ teaspoon ground cloves**
- ☐ **¹/₄ teaspoon ground cardamom**
- ☐ **¹/₄ teaspoon ground nutmeg**
- ☐ **¹/₂ teaspoon flour**
- ☐ **250 mL (8 fl.oz) chicken stock**
- ☐ **125 g (4 oz) unflavoured yoghurt**
- ☐ **125 mL (4 fl.oz) cream**

RICE PILAU
- ☐ **2 tablespoons ghee**
- ☐ **¹/₂ teaspoon ground saffron**
- ☐ **¹/₂ teaspoon ground cardamom**
- ☐ **1 teaspoon salt**
- ☐ **210 g (6¹/₂ oz) basmati rice, well washed**
- ☐ **1 L (1³/₄ pts) chicken stock**
- ☐ **2 tablespoons sultanas**
- ☐ **60 g (2 oz) chopped cashew nuts, roasted**

1 Heat ghee in a large frypan, cook onions for 2–3 minutes or until golden brown. Remove from pan and set aside.
2 Add chicken to the pan and cook until well browned on all sides. Remove from pan and set aside.
3 Combine ginger, garlic, cumin, cinnamon, cloves, cardamom, nutmeg and flour. Stir into pan and cook for 1–2 minutes. Add stock, yoghurt and cream, stirring to lift pan sediment.
4 Return chicken to the pan with half the onions. Cover and simmer for 15-20 minutes. Remove from heat and stand, covered, for 15 minutes.
5 To make rice pilau, heat ghee in a large saucepan. Cook saffron, cardamom, salt and rice for 1–2 minutes. Pour in stock and bring to the boil. Add sultanas, reduce heat and cook gently for 10–15 minutes or until most of the stock is absorbed. Cover and set aside for 10 minutes.
6 Transfer half the rice to a large ovenproof dish, top with chicken pieces, then remaining rice. Drizzle over sauce from chicken, top with remaining onions and cashew nuts. Cover and bake at 180°C (350°F) for 20–30 minutes.

MUSTARD CHILLI PORK

Perfect pork transformed into an exciting dish for a special occasion. The fiery taste of mustard and chilli is a wonderful complement to the zesty tang of lime.

Serves 4

- ☐ **750 g (1¹/₂ lb) pork fillets**
- ☐ **60 g (2 oz) melted butter**
- ☐ **30 g (1 oz) ghee**
- ☐ **2 tablespoons peanut oil**
- ☐ **3 onions, chopped**
- ☐ **1 tablespoon black mustard seeds**
- ☐ **2 cloves garlic, crushed**
- ☐ **2 red chillies, chopped**
- ☐ **¹/₂ teaspoon ground cumin**
- ☐ **¹/₂ teaspoon ground turmeric**
- ☐ **1 tablespoon brown sugar**
- ☐ **250 mL (8 fl.oz) water**
- ☐ **1 tablespoon lime juice**
- ☐ **8 kasmir lime leaves**

1 Trim meat of all visible fat, brush with melted butter and bake at 180°C (350°F) for 25–30 minutes.
2 Heat ghee and oil in a saucepan, cook onions, mustard seeds, garlic and chillies for 2-3 minutes or until onions soften.
3 Stir in cumin, turmeric, brown sugar, water, lime juice and lime leaves. Bring to the boil, then reduce heat and simmer, uncovered, for 10 minutes or until mixture reduces and thickens.
4 Transfer mixture to a food processor or blender. Process until smooth, then return to pan. Slice pork diagonally and add to mustard mixture. Heat through gently and serve.

> ### SUPERIOR SPICES
> ❖ Dry-frying whole spices before grinding mellows the flavour and will add that special touch to your cooking. Spices can be dry-fried individually or in mixtures.
> ❖ To dry-fry spices, heat a heavy-based frypan over a medium heat. Add spices and stir constantly until they are evenly browned. Be careful not to let the spices burn. Remove the spices from the pan and allow to cool before grinding.

Chicken Biryani, Mustard Chilli Pork

FIERY CHICKEN NOODLE SOUP

Serves 6

- ☐ 110 g (3½ oz) fresh egg noodles
- ☐ 2 tablespoons peanut oil
- ☐ 2 onions, chopped
- ☐ 2 cloves garlic, crushed
- ☐ 1 red chilli, finely sliced
- ☐ 1 teaspoon curry paste (vindaloo)
- ☐ ½ teaspoon powdered saffron
- ☐ 1 tablespoon finely chopped fresh lemon grass
- ☐ 1 L (1¾ pts) coconut milk
- ☐ 350 mL (11 fl.oz) chicken stock
- ☐ 375 g (12 oz) cooked chicken, finely chopped
- ☐ 3 spinach leaves, finely shredded

1   Cook noodles in a large saucepan of boiling water for 3–4 minutes or until tender. Drain and rinse noodles under cold running water. Drain and place in individual bowls.

2   Heat oil in a large saucepan, cook onions for 2–3 minutes or until golden. Stir in garlic, chilli, curry paste, saffron and lemon grass. Cook for 1 minute over medium heat.

4   Combine coconut milk and chicken stock, add to pan with chicken and spinach. Simmer for 3–4 minutes. Pour over noodles in bowls to serve.

TANDOORI BEEF RIBS

Serves 4

- ☐ 8 beef spare ribs
- ☐ 2 tablespoons peanut oil

MARINADE
- ☐ 250 g (8 oz) unflavoured yoghurt
- ☐ 1½ teaspoons grated fresh ginger
- ☐ 2 cloves garlic, crushed
- ☐ 3 teaspoons hot chilli sauce
- ☐ 1 teaspoon ground cumin
- ☐ 1 teaspoon ground cardamom
- ☐ 1 tablespoon finely chopped fresh coriander
- ☐ few drops red food colouring
- ☐ 1 tablespoon tamarind paste
- ☐ 125 mL (4 fl.oz) water

1   Trim meat of all visible fat and set aside.

2   To make marinade, combine yoghurt, ginger, garlic, chilli, cumin, cardamom, coriander and food colouring. Blend tamarind paste with water and fold into yoghurt mixture.

3   Rub marinade into meat and set aside, covered, for at least 3 hours or overnight.

4   Remove meat from marinade and brush with oil. Grill or barbecue over medium heat for 8–10 minutes, turning and basting frequently with marinade.

Left: Dry Beef Curry, Tandoori Beef Ribs,
Far left: Fiery Chicken Noodle Soup

COOK'S TIP

The secret of a good curry depends on how well the onions are browned in the first stage of cooking. Heat the oil or ghee first, add the onions and cook until golden brown. Stir gently throughout cooking being careful not to burn. Once cooked, add the spices and meat, stir to coat meat well.

❖

DRY BEEF CURRY

Serve this hot curry with plenty of yoghurt or our Cucumber Pickle (page 14) to soothe and cool the palate.

Serves 4

- ☐ **4 tablespoons, melted ghee**
- ☐ **500 g (1 lb) chuck steak, cubed**
- ☐ **1 large onion, chopped**
- ☐ **2 red chillies, finely sliced**
- ☐ **2 cloves garlic, crushed**
- ☐ **1 teaspoon ground coriander**
- ☐ **1 teaspoon ground saffron**
- ☐ **1 teaspoon ground cumin**
- ☐ **1 teaspoon black mustard seeds**
- ☐ **1 tablespoon ground garam masala**
- ☐ **125 mL (4 fl. oz) water**
- ☐ **2 large tomatoes, peeled and chopped**
- ☐ **2 curry leaves**
- ☐ **1 small cinnamon stick**
- ☐ **1 teaspoon salt**
- ☐ **3 tablespoon unflavoured yoghurt**

1   Heat 3 tablespoons ghee in a large saucepan, cook meat in batches until brown on all sides. Remove from pan and set aside

2   Heat remaining ghee in pan, add onion and chilli, cook for 2–3 minutes or until onion softens. Stir in garlic, coriander, saffron, cumin, mustard seeds and half the garam masala. Cook for 1 minute longer.

3   Combine water, tomatoes, curry leaves and cinnamon stick. Stir into pan with onion mixture. Bring to the boil, then reduce heat to simmer. Return meat to the pan and simmer for 1^1/2 hours or until meat is tender.

4   Remove pan from heat and stir in remaining garam masala, salt and yoghurt. Simmer gently for 5 minutes.

Curry Party

Surprise your guests with your versatility by making a variety of hot, mild, sweet and pungent curries, accompaniments, breads and rice dishes and (before you faint at the thought of all that work) remember that everything goes on the table at once. So, cook ahead, serve all at once, and then just sit back and enjoy yourself too.

Sambals (page 15), Chicken with Chillies (page 14),Raspberry Peach Soup, Royal Lamb Curry (page 14), Golden Rice with Coconut (page 14), Cucumber Pickle (page 14)

MENU

◆

Raspberry Peach Soup

◆

Royal Lamb Curry

◆

Chicken with Chillies

◆

Golden Rice with Coconut

◆

Cucumber Pickle

◆

Selection of Sambals

◆

Mandarin Liqueur Sorbet

❖

RASPBERRY PEACH SOUP

A refreshing soup that adds a dash of colour to your table and soothes the palate.

Serves 4

- ☐ **250 g (8 oz) fresh raspberries**
- ☐ **2 firm peaches, peeled and chopped finely**
- ☐ **2 apples, peeled, cored and chopped finely**
- ☐ **500 mL (16 fl. oz) water**
- ☐ **1 teaspoon grated lemon rind**
- ☐ **3 tablespoons lemon juice**
- ☐ **4 whole cloves**
- ☐ **1 tablespoon sugar**
- ☐ **3 tablespoons dry white wine**
- ☐ **410 g (13 oz) green grapes**
- ☐ **4 tablespoons sour cream**
- ☐ **2 tablespoons toasted slivered almonds**

1   Combine raspberries, peaches, apples, water, rind, juice and cloves in medium saucepan. Bring to the boil, reduce heat and simmer, covered, for 10 minutes. Remove cloves and set aside to cool.

2   Place fruit mixture in food processor or blender and process until smooth. Stir in sugar, wine and grapes, mix until sugar dissolves. Cover and refrigerate for 2 hours. To serve, top soup with a dollop of sour cream and sprinkle with almonds.

ROYAL LAMB CURRY

Our lamb curry is ideal for entertaining as you can make it the day before and then reheat it when required. Making curries in advance really brings out the flavour and makes entertaining easy for you.

Serves 8

- ☐ **2 tablespoons peanut oil**
- ☐ **3 onions, finely chopped**
- ☐ **2 red fresh chillies, seeds removed, and finely chopped**
- ☐ **1 clove garlic, crushed**
- ☐ **2 cardamom pods, split**
- ☐ **1 cinnamon stick**
- ☐ **2 tablespoons ground coriander**
- ☐ **2 tablespoons ground cumin**
- ☐ **1 teaspoon turmeric**
- ☐ **1 teaspoon ground nutmeg**
- ☐ **2 tablespoons lime juice**
- ☐ **1 tablespoon paprika**
- ☐ **350 g (11 oz) unflavoured yoghurt**
- ☐ **1 kg (2 lb) lean leg lamb, cubed**
- ☐ **440 g (14 oz) canned tomatoes, mashed and undrained**
- ☐ **freshly ground black pepper**

1   Heat oil in a large saucepan, cook onions, chillies, garlic, cardamom and cinnamon over a medium heat for 10 minutes, or until onions are golden and soft. Remove cardamom pods and cinnamon stick; discard.
2   Stir in coriander, cumin, turmeric and nutmeg. Cook for 4–5 minutes or until the spice mixture is dry. Stir in lime juice and cook for 1 minute longer.
3   Add paprika and gradually stir in yoghurt. Add lamb and tomatoes and season to taste with pepper. Mix well to combine all ingredients.
4   Simmer, covered, for 1 hour or until meat is tender.

CHICKEN WITH CHILLIES

A spicy chicken dish that only takes minutes to prepare. To save time, you can prepare all the ingredients in advance. For our dinner party, make double quantity of this recipe.

Serves 4

- ☐ **1 tablespoon peanut oil**
- ☐ **2 cloves garlic, crushed**
- ☐ **2 small red chillies, finely chopped**
- ☐ **500 g (1 lb) chicken breast fillets, cut into thin strips**
- ☐ **2 teaspoons fish sauce**
- ☐ **1 teaspoon light soy sauce**
- ☐ **80 mL (2^1/2 fl.oz) chicken stock**
- ☐ **4 shallots, finely chopped**
- ☐ **^{1}/2 green capsicum, finely sliced**
- ☐ **1 tablespoon chopped fresh coriander**

1   Heat oil in a wok or frypan and stir-fry garlic and chilli for 1 minute. Add chicken and stir-fry until just cooked.
2   Combine fish sauce, soy sauce and chicken stock. Pour into pan with chicken and simmer for 4-5 minutes or until chicken is tender. Stir in shallots, capsicum, and coriander, cook for 1 minute more. Remove from heat and serve immediately.

GOLDEN RICE WITH COCONUT

Coconut milk is a wonderful addition to this rice dish. It has a soothing effect when served with spicy meat and chicken dishes.

Serves 8

- ☐ **410 g (13 oz) long grain rice, washed and well drained**
- ☐ **1 L (1^3/4 pts) thin coconut milk**
- ☐ **1 teaspoon salt**
- ☐ **1 teaspoon ground turmeric**
- ☐ **2 lime leaves**
- ☐ **45 g (1^1/2 oz) desiccated coconut**
- ☐ **2 eggs, beaten**
- ☐ **2 tablespoons fried onion flakes**

1   Place rice, coconut milk, salt, turmeric, lime leaves and coconut in a heavy-based saucepan. Bring to the boil, reduce heat, cover and cook for 20 minutes or until rice has absorbed the coconut milk. Stir occasionally to prevent rice from sticking. Remove from heat and allow to stand for 10 minutes.
2   Lightly grease a wok and heat over a medium heat. Add the eggs and move back and forth until the egg sets in a thin sheet, continue to cook until firm. Roll the egg omelette up and cut into fine strips. Serve the rice topped with the shredded egg and onion flakes.

CUCUMBER PICKLE

Accompaniments to hot or spicy foods should be a combination of cool and soothing flavours. This cooling cucumber pickle is ideal with all Indian dishes.

Makes 750 mL (1^1/4 pts)

- ☐ **500 mL (16 fl. oz) white vinegar**
- ☐ **3 tablespoons lime juice**
- ☐ **1 tablespoon palm sugar**
- ☐ **^{1}/2 teaspoon salt**
- ☐ **1 teaspoon black peppercorns**
- ☐ **1 large cucumber, peeled, seeds removed and thinly sliced**
- ☐ **1 onion, sliced**
- ☐ **1 red chilli, seeds removed and chopped**

1   Place vinegar, lime juice, sugar, salt and peppercorns in a saucepan. Bring to the boil, reduce heat and cook for 1 minute.
2   Pack cucumber, onion and chilli into warm sterilised jars. Pour over warm vinegar. Seal and label when cold. Store in the refrigerator until required.

DINNER PARTY TIPS

- ❖ Cook ahead as much as possible.
- ❖ Be careful about presentation. Bowl after bowl of curry is not an appetising sight. Use the colour of coriander, the reds, greens and yellows of fresh chillies and the whites of yoghurt and breads to break up the table.
- ❖ Be mindful of offering different flavours and textures when planning your Indian Curry Party. Not everybody likes fiery curries with steamed rice. A creamy, mild chicken curry accompanied by a sweet chutney and buttery bread is sure to find strong favour with other guests.
- ❖ Vary the sizes of your bowls and plates. Put out enough serving spoons so that each dish has its own spoon.
- ❖ Put the chutneys and pickles into small containers together with a teaspoon or small fork.
- ❖ Guests can eat breads wrapped around a spoonful of curry with their fingers, or scoop up rice and curry with a fork and a dessertspoon.
- ❖ Provide napkins and fingerbowls for each guest.
- ❖ Cardamom pods are often chewed at the end of an Indian meal.
- ❖ Set the mood further by burning sticks of incense around the room, and perhaps put on some recorded sitar music as well.
- ❖ Brave hostesses might consider tackling the wearing of a sari!

SIMPLE CURRY SAMBALS

This selection of sambals is ideal to serve as part of any Indian curry party. Serve all of them for lots of variety or choose just two or three favourites.

BANANA SAMBAL

- ☐ **2 bananas, peeled and sliced**
- ☐ **1 tablespoon lemon juice**

Combine banana and lemon juice and serve.

GREEN MANGO SAMBAL

- ☐ **1 firm green mango, diced finely**
- ☐ **1 small red chilli, seeds removed and chopped**
- ☐ **1 tablespoon lemon juice**

Combine mango, chilli and lemon juice and serve.

COCONUT SAMBAL

- ☐ **60 g (2 oz) desiccated coconut**
- ☐ **1 tablespoon finely chopped onion**
- ☐ **1 small red chilli, seeds removed and chopped**
- ☐ **1 tablespoon lime juice**

Combine coconut, onion, chilli and lime juice and serve.

CUCUMBER SAMBAL

- ☐ **1 small cucumber, peeled, seeds removed and sliced thinly**
- ☐ **1 clove garlic, crushed**
- ☐ **125 g (4 oz) unflavoured yoghurt**

Combine cucumber, garlic and yoghurt and serve.

TOMATO SAMBAL

- ☐ **2 tomatoes, finely chopped**
- ☐ **1 green chilli, seeds removed and sliced**
- ☐ **1 tablespoon lemon juice**
- ☐ **1 tablespoon finely chopped onion**
- ☐ **1 tablespoon desiccated coconut**

Combine tomatoes, chilli, lemon juice and onion. Sprinkle with coconut and serve.

Mandarin Liqueur Sorbet

MANDARIN LIQUEUR SORBET

A refreshing cooling sorbet that is the perfect finish to this fiery curry party.

Serves 8

- ☐ **250 g (8 oz) caster sugar**
- ☐ **375 mL (12 fl. oz) water**
- ☐ **1.5 kg (3 lb) peeled mandarin, pith and seeds removed**
- ☐ **2 1/2 tablespoons mandarin liqueur**
- ☐ **1 large egg white**

1   Place sugar and water in a saucepan and stir over a low heat until sugar dissolves. Remove from heat and set aside until completely cold.

2   Place mandarin segments in a food processor or blender and puree. Stir in sugar syrup and liqueur. Press mixture through a sieve. Pour into a freezerproof container and freeze until semi-frozen.

3   Beat egg white until stiff peaks form. Remove sorbet mixture from freezer and fold through egg white. Return to freezer until completely frozen.

COOK'S TIP

Palm sugar is a solid ingredient which can make measuring difficult. It is easier to measure if you cut off a section and heat in a pan over hot water for a few minutes or place in the microwave and heat on HIGH (100%) for 30 seconds.

Spicy Dishes

Evoke the atmosphere of an outdoor food stall in Singapore; capture the essence of a Bangkok market or a Balinese banquet. Spices – the mere word suggests exotic images – can work miracles in the kitchen, transforming everyday, inexpensive ingredients into memorable dishes. We'll show you how easy it all is.

Spiced Duckling, Oriental Style Noodles

❖

ORIENTAL STYLE NOODLES

This sumptuous stir-fry with a touch of spice makes a complete meal in itself.

Serves 4

- ☐ **250 g (8 oz) lean minced pork**
- ☐ **250 g (8 oz) uncooked prawns, peeled and deveined**
- ☐ **250 g (8 oz) egg noodles**
- ☐ **3 tablespoons polyunsaturated oil**
- ☐ **1 onion, cut into eighths**
- ☐ **1 small red chilli, finely chopped**
- ☐ **1 large carrot, grated**
- ☐ **125 g (4 oz) bean sprouts**
- ☐ **125 mL (4 fl. oz) chicken stock**

MARINADE
- ☐ **2 tablespoons soy sauce**
- ☐ **1 tablespoon brown sugar**
- ☐ **1 tablespoon dry sherry**
- ☐ **1 tablespoon sate sauce**
- ☐ **1 teaspoon cornflour**

1　To make marinade, combine soy, brown sugar, sherry, sate sauce and cornflour in a glass bowl. Add pork and prawns and set aside to marinate for 20 minutes.

2　Place noodles in a large pan of boiling water. Cook for 5 minutes, or until just tender. Drain and set aside.

3　Heat 2 tablespoon of oil in a wok or frypan, add the pork and prawn mixture. Stir-fry for 2–3 minutes or until pork and prawns change colour. Remove from pan and set aside.

4　Heat remaining oil in pan, stir in onion and chilli, stir-fry for 2–3 minutes or until onion softens. Add noodles and pour in stock, cook until almost all the liquid is absorbed. Return pork mixture to the pan with carrot and bean sprouts. Stir-fry until heated through and serve immediately.

❖

SPICED DUCKLING

All the spices of the Orient combine to make this delicious treat.

Serves 6

- ☐ **1 L (1³/₄ pts) chicken stock**
- ☐ **125 mL (4 fl. oz) soy sauce**
- ☐ **2.5 cm (1 in) piece fresh ginger**
- ☐ **2 cloves garlic, sliced**
- ☐ **2 teaspoons five spice powder**
- ☐ **1.75 kg–2 kg (3¹/₂ lb–4 lb) duckling**
- ☐ **oil for cooking**

MARINADE
- ☐ **2 tablespoons sugar**
- ☐ **2 tablespoons dry sherry**
- ☐ **¹/₂ teaspoon five spice powder**
- ☐ **¹/₂ teaspoon sesame oil**
- ☐ **1 tablespoon soy sauce**
- ☐ **1 teaspoon chilli sauce**

1　Place stock, soy, ginger, garlic, and five spice powder in a large saucepan. Cover and bring to the boil. Add duckling and boil for 1 minute. Remove pan from heat and stand, covered, until liquid cools.

2　To make marinade, combine sugar, sherry, five spice, sesame oil, soy sauce and chilli sauce in a bowl. Remove duckling from liquid and drain well. Cut duckling in half through centre of breast bone and back bone. Pat dry with absorbent paper.

3　Place duckling halves, cut side down, on an oven tray. Rub marinade well into skin of duckling and set aside to marinate for 2 hours. Heat enough oil in a wok or frypan to cover one half of duckling. Cook until golden brown, then remove from pan and drain on absorbent paper. Repeat with remaining half. Cut duckling into serving portions with a cleaver or knife.

NOODLE KNOW-HOW

❖　When visiting an Asian or Oriental supermarket there are dozens of different types of noodles. The following is a guide to help you decide which noodles to buy.

❖　Bean thread noodles are used in both Chinese and Japanese cookery. They are the thin, translucent noodles made from the mung bean, that are simmered in soups and used in Chinese hot pots.

❖　Cellophane noodles are also known as vermicelli noodles. These are usually made from seaweed and are very fine, translucent noodles. These noodles are used in the same way as bean thread noodles.

❖　Chinese egg noodles are sold fresh or dry, fresh is best if you have a choice. They are available as wide or narrow noodles.

❖　Rice sticks are long thin noodles used in Chinese and Southeast Asian cookery. A favourite way of cooking them is to fry them. When added to oil they increase their volume by six and become light and crisp.

❖　Wheat noodles are similar to egg noodles, but are made from just flour and water and are usually flat.

SKEWERED PORK

Our marinated pork has an exquisite flavour and is especially good if cooked on a barbecue.

Serves 4

☐ **750 g (1¹/₂ lb) pork fillets, sliced**

MARINADE
☐ **1 teaspoon grated fresh ginger**
☐ **1 onion, finely chopped**
☐ **5 tablespoons Japanese soy sauce**
☐ **3 tablespoons brown sugar**
☐ **4 tablespoons dry sherry**

1 To make marinade, place ginger, onion, soy, brown sugar and sherry in a glass bowl. Add pork and toss well to coat. Set aside to marinate for 1 hour.
2 Remove pork from marinade and thread onto eight oiled skewers. Grill or barbecue for 6–8 minutes, basting with marinade and turning frequently. Serve immediately.

SPICED FRIED CALAMARI

The secret of this dish is the marinade. The longer you can leave the calamari to marinate the better the flavour will be.

Serves 4

☐ **500 g (1 lb) calamari rings**

MARINADE
☐ **2 teaspoons tamarind paste**
☐ **¹/₄ teaspoon ground saffron**
☐ **1 teaspoon grated fresh ginger**
☐ **2 cloves garlic, crushed**
☐ **1 tablespoon teriyaki sauce**
☐ **90 mL (3 fl. oz) polyunsaturated oil**

BATTER
☐ **155 g (5 oz) plain flour**
☐ **80 mL (2¹/₂ fl. oz) water**
☐ **1 egg, beaten**
☐ **freshly ground black pepper**

1 To make marinade, combine tamarind paste, saffron, ginger, garlic, teriyaki sauce and oil in a glass bowl. Add calamari rings and set aside for 30 minutes.
2 To make batter, place flour in a mixing bowl. Gradually stir in water, then egg. Season to taste with pepper. Drain calamari and dip into batter.
3 Heat the oil in a wok or frypan and cook the calamari until golden brown and crisp. Drain on absorbent paper and serve.

COOKING CALAMARI

✦ The main rule to remember when cooking calamari or squid is that the cooking time is either very brief or very long, anything in between will be tough.
✦ Marinating large squid for several hours, in a mixture of lemon or lime jucie, onion and fresh herbs will not only add flavour, but will ensure a tender dish.
✦ On young calamari, the most delicate parts are the tentacles, which are delicious dipped in batter and quickly fried.

EGGPLANT WITH CHILLI AND CINNAMON

Serve this wonderful fusion of eggplant, tomatoes and spices with brown rice and plenty of unflavoured yoghurt.

Serves 4

☐ **60 mL (2 fl. oz) peanut oil**
☐ **1 large onion, sliced**
☐ **4 cloves garlic, crushed**
☐ **1 small red chilli, finely chopped**
☐ **1 teaspoon ground coriander**
☐ **1 teaspoon salt**
☐ **1 teaspoon black mustard seeds**
☐ **2 large eggplant, chopped into 2.5 cm (1 in) cubes**
☐ **440 g (14 oz) canned tomatoes, undrained and mashed**
☐ **125 mL (4 fl. oz) chicken stock**
☐ **2.5 cm (1 in) piece of cinnamon stick**

1 Heat oil in a large saucepan, cook onion for 2–3 minutes or until golden. Add garlic, chilli, coriander, salt and mustard seeds and cook for 1 minute.
2 Toss in eggplant and stir-fry for 1–2 minutes. Combine tomatoes, stock and cinnamon stick. Pour into pan with eggplant mixture. Bring to the boil, reduce heat and simmer for 25–30 minutes or until eggplant is tender and mixture thickens.

Skewered Pork, Spiced Fried Calamari, Eggplant with Chilli and Cinnamon

BEEF AND PICKLED VEGETABLE OMELETTE

The Chinese mixed vegetables used as the filling for this omelette are available from most Oriental supermarkets.

Serves 4

- ☐ 2 tablespoons peanut oil
- ☐ 250 g (8 oz) lean minced beef
- ☐ 2 tablespoons bottled Chinese mixed vegetables (tung chai), drained and chopped
- ☐ 1 teaspoon honey
- ☐ 2 tablespoons soy sauce
- ☐ 6 shallots, finely chopped
- ☐ 6 eggs, lightly beaten

1   Heat half the oil in a frypan, add mince, vegetables, honey, soy and shallots, stir-fry for 3–4 minutes. Remove from pan, set aside and keep warm.

2   Heat remaining oil in a clean frypan. Pour in quarter of the beaten eggs. Swirl pan over heat to make a thin omelette.

3   Spoon quarter of the meat mixture into the centre of the omelette and fold over the edges.

4   Remove from pan and keep warm. Repeat with remaining eggs and meat mixture. Cut omelettes into slices and serve.

Beef and Pickled Vegetable Omelette

LAMB WITH GINGER AND HONEY

Lamb, ginger and honey are a wonderful combination in this timesaving treat.

Serves 4

- ☐ 2 tablespoons peanut oil
- ☐ 3 cloves garlic, crushed
- ☐ 1 tablespoon grated fresh ginger
- ☐ 500 g (1 lb) lean lamb steaks, cut into thin strips
- ☐ 1 onion, cut into eighths
- ☐ 210 g (6$\frac{1}{2}$ oz) oyster mushrooms, sliced
- ☐ 155 g (5 oz) snow peas
- ☐ 2 tablespoons soy sauce
- ☐ 1 tablespoon honey
- ☐ 2 teaspoons lime juice

1   Heat half the oil in a frypan or wok and stir-fry garlic and ginger for a few seconds. Add meat in batches and stir-fry for 2–3 minutes each batch. Remove from pan and set aside.

2   Heat remaining oil and cook onion, mushrooms and snow peas for 2–3 minutes. Return meat to the pan with vegetables and stir-fry for 1 minute.

3   Combine soy sauce, honey and lime juice and add to the pan. Stir-fry for 1–2 minutes more or until heated through. Serve immediately.

LOVELY LEMON GRASS

Lemon grass is used extensively in Sri Lankan and Southeast Asian cookery. It is used to flavour curry, meat and fish dishes as well as sweet desserts. Lemon grass is available from Asian supermarkets in both the fresh and dried forms. There is also a powdered form available which is called sereh, this is strong in flavour and should be used with discretion. If lemon grass is unavailable lemon balm, lemon verbena or lemon rind are possible substitutes.

❖

CHICKEN WITH AROMATIC SPICES AND CASHEWS

The addition of coconut milk to aromatic spices gives this quick curry a special touch.

Serves 4

- [ ] **1 onion, finely chopped**
- [ ] **2 cloves garlic, crushed**
- [ ] **$^1/_2$ teaspoon sugar**
- [ ] **$^1/_2$ teaspoon black mustard seeds**
- [ ] **$^1/_2$ teaspoon curry paste**
- [ ] **pinch chilli powder**
- [ ] **1 teaspoon fish sauce**
- [ ] **1 tablespoon lime juice**
- [ ] **500 g (1 lb) chicken pieces**
- [ ] **1 tablespoon peanut oil**
- [ ] **1 stalk lemon grass, finely chopped**
- [ ] **250 mL (8 fl. oz) coconut cream**
- [ ] **125 mL (4 fl. oz) water**
- [ ] **3 tablespoons chopped roasted cashews**

1   Combine onion, garlic, sugar, mustard seeds, curry paste, chilli powder, fish sauce and lime juice in a glass bowl. Add chicken, toss well and set aside to marinate for 30 minutes.

2   Heat oil in a large frypan and stir-fry lemon grass for a few seconds. Add the chicken mixture to the pan and cook for 4–5 minutes each side.

3   Stir in the coconut cream and water. Simmer for 15–20 minutes or until chicken is tender and sauce thickens. To serve, top with cashews.

Chicken with Aromatic Spices and Cashews
Lamb with Ginger and Honey

SPICED PORK AND VEGETABLE SOUP

Serve this rich soup as a first course or as part of a main course with other dishes.

Serves 4

- [ ] **250 g (8 oz) lean pork steaks, cut into strips**
- [ ] **2 teaspoons soy sauce**
- [ ] **1 tablespoon cornflour**
- [ ] **1 teaspoon sherry**
- [ ] **2 tablespoons peanut oil**
- [ ] **1 large carrot, cut into thin strips**
- [ ] **1 stick celery, cut into thin strips**
- [ ] **110 g (3¹/₂ oz) oyster mushrooms, sliced**
- [ ] **1.5 L (2¹/₂ pts) chicken stock**
- [ ] **2 teaspoons chilli sauce**
- [ ] **freshly ground black pepper**
- [ ] **6 shallots, cut into 2.5 cm (1 in) lengths**
- [ ] **¹/₂ cucumber, cut into thin strips**
- [ ] **45 g (1¹/₂ oz) transparent noodles**

1   Combine pork, soy sauce, cornflour and sherry in a glass bowl. Set aside to marinate for 20 minutes.

2   Heat oil in a large saucepan, stir-fry pork for 2–3 minutes. Remove from pan and keep warm. Add carrot, celery and mushrooms, stir-fry for 1–2 minutes.

3   Combine stock, chilli sauce and pepper, pour over meat and vegetables in pan. Bring to the boil, reduce heat and simmer for 10 minutes.

4   Add pork, shallots, cucumber and noodles, cook for 3–4 minutes more. Ladle into individual bowls and serve immediately.

BEEF IN COCONUT MILK

A thick, spicy sauce coats the meat and makes for a satisfying meal.

Serves 4

- [ ] **2 onions, chopped**
- [ ] **1 tablespoon sambal oelek**
- [ ] **3 tablespoons chopped macadamia nuts**
- [ ] **¹/₂ teaspoon dried shrimp paste**
- [ ] **250 mL (8 fl. oz) water**
- [ ] **2 tablespoons peanut oil**
- [ ] **500 g (1 lb) lean topside steak, cut into 2.5cm (1in) cubes**
- [ ] **250 mL (8 fl. oz) coconut milk**
- [ ] **1 tablespoon mango chutney**
- [ ] **2 tablespoons lime juice**

1   Place onions, sambal oelek, nuts, shrimp paste and 1 tablespoon of water in a food processor or blender and process until smooth.

2   Heat oil in a saucepan. Add the onion mixture and cook gently for 3–4 minutes, stirring frequently. Stir in the meat and cook for 2–3 minutes or until meat changes colour and is well-coated in onion mixture.

3   Pour in remaining water, cover and simmer for 1 hour or until meat is tender. Combine coconut milk, chutney and lime juice, add to pan with meat mixture. Simmer, uncovered, for 10–15 minutes, stirring occasionally.

ZESTY GREEN BEANS

A simple yet delicious way of cooking green beans, that goes well with Indian meals and with grilled and roasted meats. For a milder dish, you can leave out the chilli.

Serves 4

- [ ] **500 g (1 lb) fresh green beans, trimmed**
- [ ] **3 tablespoons peanut oil**
- [ ] **1 onion, chopped**
- [ ] **1 tablespoon yellow mustard seeds**
- [ ] **4 cloves garlic, crushed**
- [ ] **1 small red chilli, finely chopped**
- [ ] **¹/₂ teaspoon sugar**
- [ ] **¹/₄ teaspoon cayenne pepper**
- [ ] **2 tablespoons lemon juice**

1   Boil, steam or microwave beans until just tender. Drain and refresh under cold running water. Pat dry with absorbent paper and set aside.

2   Heat oil in a frypan, cook onion for 2–3 minutes or until golden. Add mustard seeds, garlic and chilli, stir-fry for 1 minute.

3   Toss in beans, sugar and cayenne. Stir-fry for 2–3 minutes or until heated. Stir in lemon juice and serve immediately.

SPICY VEGETABLES

Use any vegetables you like for this dish, but we find this combination perfect. Remember not to overcook your vegetable selection when stir-frying or they will become soggy and lose much of their valuable vitamins!

Serves 4

- [ ] **3 tablespoons peanut oil**
- [ ] **2 onions, cut into eighths**
- [ ] **1 teaspoon grated fresh ginger**
- [ ] **210 g (6¹/₂ oz) oyster mushrooms, sliced**
- [ ] **1 small head broccoli, broken into florets**
- [ ] **¹/₂ chinese cabbage, shredded**
- [ ] **1 large carrot, cut into thin strips**
- [ ] **2 stalks celery, sliced diagonally**
- [ ] **250 g (8 oz) snow peas**
- [ ] **60 mL (2 fl. oz) chicken stock**

SAUCE
- [ ] **1 tablespoon sesame oil**
- [ ] **1 tablespoon soy sauce**
- [ ] **2 teaspoons honey**
- [ ] **1 teaspoon lemon juice**

1   Heat oil in a wok or frypan, stir-fry onions for 2–3 minutes or until golden. Add ginger and mushrooms. Stir-fry for 1 minute more.

2   Add broccoli, cabbage, carrot, celery, snow peas and stock. Stir-fry for 2–3 minutes or until vegetables are just tender.

3   To make sauce, combine sesame oil, soy sauce, honey and lemon juice. Pour over vegetables in pan and stir-fry until heated through. Serve immediately.

COCONUT MILK

✦   Coconut milk can be purchased in a number of forms – canned, as a long-life product in cartons or as a powder to which you add water. Once opened it has a short life and should be used within a day or so.

✦   You can also make coconut milk using desiccated coconut and water. To make coconut milk, place 500 g (1 lb) of desiccated coconut in a bowl and pour over 750 mL (1¹/₂ pts) of boiling water. Leave to stand for 30 minutes, strain squeezing the coconut to extract as much liquid as possible. This will make a thick coconut milk. The coconut can be used again to make a weaker coconut milk.

Beef in Coconut Milk, Spiced Pork and Vegetable Soup, Zesty Green Beans, Spicy Vegetables

Light Dishes

Nuts, fruits, vegetables, herbs and small amounts of meat are the ingredients. Steaming, braising, stir-frying and slow baking are the cooking methods. Welcome to light cooking, where "less is more" and tastes are sensational. What a relief that pared down, light cooking and eating is so fashionable – it's simply delicious.

Thai Beef Salad, Cinnamon Glazed Pawpaw, Spiced Almond Seafood (page 26)

THAI BEEF SALAD

Freezing the meat for 30 minutes before slicing ensures that you can cut it into the paper thin slices required for this dish.

Serves 4

- ☐ **500 g (1lb) piece rump steak**
- ☐ **2 tablespoons oil**
- ☐ **1 onion, sliced**
- ☐ **1 clove garlic, sliced**
- ☐ **1 red chilli, sliced**
- ☐ **2 tablespoons lime juice**
- ☐ **1 teaspoon sugar**
- ☐ **2 tablespoons soy sauce**
- ☐ **2 tablespoons chopped fresh mint**
- ☐ **185 g (6 oz) can water chestnuts, drained, sliced**
- ☐ **1 cucumber, sliced thinly**
- ☐ **sliced tomatoes**
- ☐ **shredded Chinese cabbage**

1 Cut meat into paper thin slices. Heat oil in wok, add meat, cook over high heat for 8 minutes or until meat is browned and all liquid is evaporated. Add onion, garlic and chilli, cook for 2 minutes longer. Transfer meat mixture to a bowl.

2 Combine juice, sugar and soy sauce in small bowl. Pour over meat. Stir in mint, chestnuts and cucumber, refrigerate for 1 hour. Serve with tomatoes and Chinese cabbage.

CINNAMON GLAZED PAWPAW

Pawpaw complements the flavour of fish, shellfish or chicken very well. For this dish, choose a semi-ripe pawpaw to ensure that it retains it's shape when baked.

Serves 6

- ☐ **¹/₂ teaspoon cinnamon**
- ☐ **2 tablespoons brown sugar**
- ☐ **1 large firm pawpaw, cut in half, seeded and peeled**
- ☐ **30 g (1 oz) butter**

1 Combine cinnamon and brown sugar and sprinkle over pawpaw. Top pawpaw with small knobs of butter.

2 Place on a baking tray and bake at 120°C (250°F) for 20 minutes or until golden and soft. To serve, cut into wedges.

SPICED ALMOND SEAFOOD

Try our Cinnamon Glazed Pawpaw for an interesting and unusual side dish to accompany this spicy seafood curry.

Serves 4

- ☐ **375 g (12 oz) medium uncooked prawns**
- ☐ **2 calamari tubes, skinned and cut into rings**
- ☐ **2 tablespoons tomato paste**
- ☐ **1 tablespoon sambal oelek**
- ☐ **2 tablespoons ghee**
- ☐ **2 onions, sliced**
- ☐ **2 teaspoons coriander seeds, crushed**
- ☐ **$^1/_2$ teaspoon ground cumin**
- ☐ **$^1/_2$ teaspoon garam masala**
- ☐ **6 dried curry leaves**
- ☐ **3 tablespoons slivered almonds**
- ☐ **8 uncooked mussels**
- ☐ **1 tablespoon brown vinegar**
- ☐ **350 mL (11 fl. oz) coconut milk**

1   Combine prawns, calamari, tomato paste and sambal oelek in a bowl.
2   Heat ghee in a large frypan, add onions, coriander, cumin, garam masala, curry leaves and almonds, stir over low heat for 3–4 minutes or until onions are soft.
3   Stir in prawn mixture and cook over high heat for 2 minutes longer. Add mussels, vinegar and milk. Bring to the boil, reduce heat and simmer, uncovered, for 5 minutes or until seafood is just cooked through.

❖

SWEET POTATO CRISPS

Spicy hot crisps, made from sweet potato. What could be more enjoyable to serve with drinks before an Asian inspired meal?

Serves 4

- ☐ **500 g (1lb) sweet potato, peeled**
- ☐ **2 tablespoons lemon juice**
- ☐ **oil for deep frying**
- ☐ **1 tablespoon salt**
- ☐ **1 teaspoon Mexican chilli powder**
- ☐ **$^1/_2$ teaspoon caster sugar**

1   Slice potatoes into paper thin slices. Place potato and lemon juice in large bowl, cover with cold water and refrigerate for 2 hours. Drain on absorbent kitchen paper.
2   Heat oil in large saucepan, cook potatoes a few at a time over medium heat for 6 minutes or until potatoes are golden and almost crisp. Remove crisps from oil, set aside and keep warm. Repeat with remaining potatoes.
3   Return cooked potatoes to hot oil and cook until crisp. Remove from oil and drain on absorbent paper. Combine salt, chilli powder and sugar, sprinkle over crisps. Serve immediately.

❖

CHICKEN WITH LEMON GRASS AND LYCHEES

A colourful and fragrant dish that only takes minutes to prepare.

Serves 6

- ☐ **oil for deep frying**
- ☐ **500 g (1lb) skinned chicken thigh fillets, chopped**
- ☐ **3 shallots, chopped**

BATTER
- ☐ **75 g (2$^1/_2$ oz) cornflour**
- ☐ **3 egg whites, lightly beaten**
- ☐ **$^1/_2$ teaspoon ground Chinese five spice**

SAUCE
- ☐ **2 teaspoons cornflour**
- ☐ **1 tablespoon soy sauce**
- ☐ **410 g (13 oz) can lychees in light syrup**
- ☐ **1 red capsicum, chopped**
- ☐ **1 green capsicum, chopped**
- ☐ **1 yellow capsicum, chopped**
- ☐ **3 tablespoons chopped fresh lemon grass**

1   To make batter, combine cornflour, egg whites and spice in small bowl. Whisk until smooth. Toss chicken in batter.
2   Heat oil in wok or frypan and cook chicken in small batches until golden and cooked through. Drain, set aside and keep warm. Repeat with remaining chicken.
3   To make sauce, blend cornflour with soy sauce in large saucepan. Stir in undrained lychees, capsicums and lemon grass. Cook over low heat until mixture thickens slightly. Stir in chicken and shallots, heat until just warmed through. Serve immediately.

Sweet Potato Crisps, Chicken with Lemon Grass and Lychees, Pork and Plum Noodles, Citrus Glazed Pork Ribs

PORK AND PLUM NOODLES

Serves 8

- ☐ **2 tablespoons oil**
- ☐ **500 g (1lb) Chinese barbecued pork, sliced thinly**
- ☐ **2 sticks celery, sliced diagonally**
- ☐ **2 tablespoons pecan nuts**
- ☐ **220 g (7 oz) bean sprouts**
- ☐ **410 g (13 oz) canned baby corn, drained, halved**
- ☐ **375 g (12 oz) Chinese egg noodles, cooked**
- ☐ **220 g (7 oz) broccoli, chopped**

SAUCE
- ☐ **1 tablespoon cornflour**
- ☐ **185 mL (6 fl. oz) chicken stock**
- ☐ **125 mL (4 fl. oz) plum sauce**
- ☐ **125 mL (4 fl. oz) hoisin sauce**

1   Heat oil in wok or frypan. Add pork, celery and nuts and cook over medium heat for 1 minute. Stir in sprouts, corn and noodles, cook over medium heat for 2 minutes longer.

2   To make sauce, combine cornflour, stock, plum sauce and hoisin sauce. Add sauce mixture and broccoli to pan, cook over high heat for 2 minutes or until sauce thickens and all ingredients are coated.

❖

CITRUS GLAZED PORK RIBS

Serves 6

- ☐ **1 kg (2 lb) back pork ribs**

GLAZE
- ☐ **250 mL (8 fl. oz) orange juice**
- ☐ **3 tablespoons lime juice**
- ☐ **2 tablespoons lemon juice**
- ☐ **1 tablespoon shredded lime rind**
- ☐ **1 tablespoon shredded lemon rind**
- ☐ **2 tablespoons brown sugar**
- ☐ **2 tablespoons wholegrain mustard**
- ☐ **1 tablespoon cornflour**
- ☐ **1 tablespoon chopped fresh lemon thyme**

1   To make glaze, combine orange, lime and lemon juices, lime and lemon rind, sugar, mustard, cornflour and thyme in a large bowl. Add ribs and toss to coat.

2   Transfer ribs and glaze to a large baking dish, bake at 220°C (425°F) for 25 minutes or until ribs are browned and well glazed, turning ribs occasionally.

SESAME PRAWN BALLS

These delicious morsels make a perfect light meal that would be ideal for a luncheon.

Serves 6

- ☐ 1 kg (2 lb) medium uncooked prawns, shelled and deveined
- ☐ 1 onion, chopped finely
- ☐ 1/2 teaspoon garam masala
- ☐ 1/4 teaspoon ground turmeric
- ☐ 185 g (6 oz) rice flour
- ☐ 1 teaspoon sesame oil
- ☐ 15 g (1/2 oz) finely chopped fresh coriander
- ☐ 3 tablespoons sesame seeds
- ☐ oil for deep frying
- ☐ shredded lettuce

SAUCE
- ☐ 1 tablespoon cornflour
- ☐ 250 mL (8 fl oz) chicken stock
- ☐ 125 mL (4 fl oz) prepared tamarind sauce
- ☐ 2 tablespoons soy sauce
- ☐ 1 tablespoon lime juice
- ☐ 1 tablespoon finely chopped coriander

1 Place prawns, onion and spices in food processor or blender and process until smooth. Stir in ground rice, oil and coriander. Cover and refrigerate mixture for 1 hour. Using wet hands, roll mixture into small balls, then roll in seeds. Refrigerate for 1 hour.

2 To make sauce, blend cornflour with stock in saucepan. Stir in tamarind sauce, soy sauce, lime juice and coriander. Bring to the boil, stirring constantly, reduce heat and simmer, uncovered, for 5 minutes.

3 Heat oil in a large saucepan. Cook balls until golden and cooked through. Serve balls on a bed of shredded lettuce with sauce spooned over.

❖

BEEF AND VEGETABLE LETTUCE CUPS

These tasty lettuce cups make an attractive entertaining dish. The filling can be made up in advance then reheated just before placing in the lettuce cups.

Serves 8

- ☐ 1 tablespoon olive oil
- ☐ 500 g (1 ib) minced beef
- ☐ 1 teaspoon ground cinnamon
- ☐ 1 teaspoon ground turmeric
- ☐ 1 teaspoon ground sweet paprika
- ☐ 2 tablespoons chopped fresh mint
- ☐ 2 tablespoons chopped fresh parsley
- ☐ 3 tablespoons tomato paste
- ☐ 125 mL (4 fl. oz) red wine
- ☐ 125 mL (4 fl. oz) beef stock
- ☐ 410 g (13 oz) canned red kidney beans, drained and rinsed
- ☐ 2 tablespoons chopped pimento
- ☐ 2 red spanish onions, sliced
- ☐ 250 g (8 oz) baby yellow squash, chopped
- ☐ 250 g (8 oz) snow peas, sliced diagonally
- ☐ 8 large lettuce cups, washed, drained

1 Heat oil in large frypan or wok. Add beef and cook over high heat for 10 minutes or until meat is well browned and all the liquid has evaporated. Stir in cinnamon, turmeric, paprika, mint, parsley, tomato paste, wine, stock, beans and pimento, cook over medium heat for 5 minutes.

2 Stir in onions, squash and snow peas. Cook until vegetables are crisp but tender, and almost all liquid has evaporated. Spoon beef and vegetables into lettuce cups. Serve immediately.

Sesame Prawn Balls, Beef and Vegetable Lettuce Cups

LEMON ROSEMARY KEBABS

If cooking kebabs on a barbecue, place branches of rosemary on the coals. This gives a rosemary flavour to the kebabs and a sweet smell to your barbecue area.

Serves 8

- ☐ **1.5 kg (3 lb) leg lamb, boned and cut into 2.5cm (1in) cubes**
- ☐ **1 red capsicum, cut into 2.5cm (1in) cubes**
- ☐ **1 green capsicum, cut into 2.5cm (1in) cubes**
- ☐ **500 g (1lb) whole button mushrooms**

MARINADE
- ☐ **125 mL (4 fl. oz) lemon juice**
- ☐ **2 tablespoons honey, warmed**
- ☐ **1 tablespoon soy sauce**
- ☐ **1 teaspoon cracked black pepper**
- ☐ **2 teaspoons dried rosemary leaves**
- ☐ **2 cloves garlic, crushed**

1 To make marinade, combine lemon juice, honey, soy sauce, pepper, rosemary and garlic in a large bowl. Add meat, toss to coat. Cover and refrigerate for 2–4 hours or overnight.

2 Thread lamb, capsicums and mushrooms alternately onto bamboo skewers. Reserve any remaining marinade. Grill or barbecue over high heat until meat is browned and cooked through. Brush occasionally with marinade during cooking.

❖

PRAWN AND SQUID SOUP

If pork bones are unavailable, replace the bones and water with a good homemade chicken stock.

Serves 6

- ☐ **500 g (1lb) smoked pork bones**
- ☐ **1.8 L (3 pts) water**
- ☐ **1 stalk lemongrass, bruised**
- ☐ **250 g (8 oz) squid tubes, cut into thin rings**
- ☐ **375 g (12 oz) medium uncooked prawns, shelled and deveined**
- ☐ **2 tablespoons fish sauce**
- ☐ **2 red chillies, sliced thinly**
- ☐ **2 shallots, chopped**
- ☐ **2 tablespoons chopped fresh coriander**
- ☐ **3 tablespoons lime juice**

1 Combine pork bones, water and lemon grass in a large saucepan. Bring to the boil, reduce heat and simmer, uncovered, for 20 minutes. Discard bones and lemon grass.

2 Stir in squid, prawns, fish sauce and chillies. Bring to the boil, reduce heat and simmer, uncovered, for 5 minutes. Stir in shallots, coriander and lime juice. Serve immediately.

Lemon Rosemary Kebabs, Prawn and Squid Soup

BACON AND VEGETABLE ROLLS

Spring rolls are one of the most popular dishes in Oriental cuisine. Our tasty adaptation is sure to be a hit. Cooked rolls can be frozen and then reheated at 180°C (350°F) for 20 minutes or until heated through.

Serves 6

- ☐ **4 rashers bacon, chopped finely**
- ☐ **2 cups finely shredded cabbage**
- ☐ **1 carrot, grated coarsely**
- ☐ **1 stick celery, finely chopped**
- ☐ **1¹/₂ teaspoons caraway seeds**
- ☐ **3 hard-boiled eggs, chopped**
- ☐ **3 tablespoons sour cream**
- ☐ **12 x 16 cm (6¹/₂) square spring roll wrappers**
- ☐ **oil for deep frying**

SAUCE
- ☐ **4 tablespoons brown vinegar**
- ☐ **2 tablespoons brown sugar**
- ☐ **1 tablespoon soy sauce**
- ☐ **1 fresh red chilli, finely chopped**

1   Cook bacon in medium pan over high heat until crisp, stir in cabbage and cook for 1 minute. Combine bacon and cabbage, carrot, celery, caraway seeds, eggs and cream in a bowl. Divide mixture into 12 portions. Spoon 1 portion of mixture diagonally across centre of each wrapper. Roll pastry up and fold in edges to form a long roll. Moisten edges of wrapper with water to seal.

2   Heat oil in a large saucepan. Cook 2 or 3 rolls at a time, in hot oil for 3 minutes or until rolls are crisp and golden. Remove from oil and drain on absorbent kitchen paper.

3   To make sauce, combine vinegar, sugar, soy sauce and chilli in small saucepan. Heat over low heat until just warmed through. Serve with rolls.

FRUIT AND NUT PORK BALLS

Tasty fruit and nut meatballs with a Middle Eastern flavour are perfect served as a light meal or as a snack with drinks.

Serves 4

- ☐ **500 g (1 ib) ground pork mince**
- ☐ **125 g (4 oz) dried apricots, finely chopped**
- ☐ **90 g (3 oz) sultanas**
- ☐ **375 g (12 oz) fresh breadcrumbs**
- ☐ **1 egg, lightly beaten**
- ☐ **1 teaspoon ground cumin**
- ☐ **2 tablespoons smooth peanut butter**
- ☐ **1 tablespoon hoisin sauce**
- ☐ **125 g (4 oz) chopped roasted peanuts**

DIPPING SAUCE
- ☐ **125 mL (4 fl. oz) light sour cream**
- ☐ **3 tablespoons fruit chutney**

1   Combine mince with apricots, sultanas, breadcrumbs, egg, cumin, peanut butter and sauce, mix well. Shape 2 tablespoonfuls of mixture into balls and roll in nuts. Refrigerate for 1 hour.

2   Place meatballs in a lightly oiled baking dish and bake at 200°C (400°F) for 25–30 minutes or until golden and cooked through.

3   To make sauce, combine sour cream and chutney. Serve as dipping sauce with meatballs.

PAPRIKA AND SESAME CHICKEN

Served with a dipping sauce, these tasty chicken wings are great finger food.

Serves 8

- ☐ **1 kg (2 lb) chicken wings, each wing cut into 2 portions**
- ☐ **1 teaspoon sesame oil**
- ☐ **2 teaspoons ground mild paprika**
- ☐ **2 teaspoons cracked black pepper**
- ☐ **2 teaspoons grated lemon rind**
- ☐ **1 teaspoon ground ginger**
- ☐ **oil for deep frying**

BATTER
- ☐ **2 egg whites, lightly beaten**
- ☐ **125 g (4 oz) cornflour, sifted**
- ☐ **4 tablespoons sesame seeds**

1   Combine chicken, oil, paprika, pepper, rind and ginger in large bowl. Refrigerate for 1 hour. To make batter, combine egg white, cornflour and seeds in medium bowl.

2   Heat oil in wok or deep frypan. Dip each chicken piece into batter. Cook chicken in hot oil until golden brown and crisp, but not cooked through. Transfer chicken to a rack, placed over a baking dish. Bake at 200°C (400°F) for 20 minutes or until chicken is cooked through.

OREGANO LAMB WITH VEGETABLES

When preparing this recipe you will need to cook 250 g (8 oz) of raw pasta to give the required cooked quantity. For variety, use some of the more interesting shapes such as spirals or shells.

Serves 4

- ☐ **5 lamb chump chops, boned, chopped into small strips**
- ☐ **2 tablespoons olive oil**
- ☐ **2 carrots, peeled, chopped**
- ☐ **1 zucchini, chopped**
- ☐ **3 cups cooked pasta**
- ☐ **3 shallots, chopped**
- ☐ **125 g (4 oz) firm black olives**
- ☐ **125 mL (4 fl. oz) cream**
- ☐ **freshly grated Parmesan cheese**

MARINADE
- ☐ **1 tablespoon chopped fresh oregano**
- ☐ **3 tablespoons lemon juice**
- ☐ **2 cloves garlic, crushed**
- ☐ **pinch cayenne pepper**

1   To make marinade, combine oregano, lemon juice, garlic and pepper in bowl. Add lamb, toss well and set aside to marinate for 1 hour.

2   Heat oil in medium saucepan. Add meat and cook over high heat for 4 minutes. Add carrot and zucchini and cook over high heat for 3 minutes longer. Stir in pasta, shallots, olives and cream. Bring to the boil, reduce heat and simmer for 5 minutes, stirring occasionally during cooking. Serve with bowls of Parmesan cheese.

Bacon and Vegetable Rolls, Fruit and Nut Pork Balls, Paprika and Sesame Chicken, Oregano Lamb with Vegetables

PERFECT RICE

METHOD	WHITE RICE	BROWN RICE
RAPID BOIL	Bring 2 L (3¹/₄ pts) water to the boil. Stir in 220 g (7 oz) rice, season to taste. Return to boil and boil rapidly for 12–15 minutes. Drain through a sieve or colander and serve.	Bring 2 L (3¹/₄ pts) water to the boil. Slowly stir in 220 g (7 oz) rice, season to taste. Stir several times with a fork and boil rapidly for 30–40 minutes. Drain and serve.
ABSORPTION	Bring 375 mL (12 fl.oz) water to the boil. Stir in 220 g (7 oz) rice. Cover and simmer for 20–25 minutes. Uncover, toss with a fork and stand for a few minutes before serving.	Bring 500 mL (1 pt) water to the boil. Stir in 220 g (7 oz) rice, season to taste. Cover and simmer for 55 minutes or until all the liquid is absorbed. Toss with a fork and serve.
MICROWAVE	Place 220 g (7 oz) rice and 500 mL water in a large microwave-safe container. Cook, uncovered, on HIGH (100%) for 12–15 minutes or until liquid is absorbed. Cover and stand for 5 minutes. Toss with a fork and serve.	Place 220 g (7 oz) rice and 750 mL water in a large microwave-safe container. Cook, uncovered, on HIGH (100%) for 30–35 minutes or until liquid is absorbed, stir during cooking. Cover and stand for 5 minutes. Toss with a fork and serve.

ROSE SCENTED SAFFRON RICE

Serve this fragrant rice accompaniment with chicken or lamb. Rosewater is available from most health food stores.

Serves 6

- [ ] **500 g (1 lb) basmati rice, well washed**
- [ ] **60 g (2 oz) ghee**
- [ ] **1 onion, chopped**
- [ ] **250 g (8 oz) minced lamb**
- [ ] **$^1/_2$ teaspoon mixed spice**
- [ ] **60 g (2 oz) currants**
- [ ] **$^1/_2$ teaspoon powdered saffron**
- [ ] **2 tablespoons rosewater**
- [ ] **1 L (1$^3/_4$ pts) chicken stock**
- [ ] **60 g (2 oz) blanched almonds, toasted**

1   Place rice in a large bowl, cover with cold water and set aside for 30 minutes.
2   Heat ghee in a heavy-based frypan, add onion and cook for 5 minutes or until onion softens. Increase heat, add lamb and cook until lamb is browned. Stir in mixed spice and currants, cook for a further minute, remove pan from heat. Set aside and keep warm.
3   Combine saffron and rosewater. Place chicken stock and 2 teaspoons of rosewater mixture in a large saucepan, bring to the boil. Drain rice and add to the stock. Bring back to the boil, stirring occasionally. Reduce heat, cover and simmer gently for 30 minutes.
4   Fold meat mixture through rice, remove from heat and stand for 5 minutes before serving. To serve, sprinkle with remaining rosewater mixture and top with almonds.

❖

PILAF WITH EGGPLANT

Pilaf is a wonderful accompaniment that could easily be a meal on its own. This version with eggplant is particularly tasty and is great served with unflavoured yoghurt.

Serves 6

- [ ] **2 eggplants, cut into 2.5cm (1in) cubes**
- [ ] **salt**
- [ ] **60 mL (2 fl. oz) olive oil**
- [ ] **1 onion, sliced**
- [ ] **440 g (14 oz) canned tomatoes, drained and chopped**
- [ ] **2 tablespoons chopped fresh parsley**

- [ ] **1 tablespoon chopped fresh mint**
- [ ] **500 g (1 lb) long grain rice, well washed**
- [ ] **750 mL (1$^1/_4$ pts) chicken stock**

1   Sprinkle eggplant with salt and set aside for 30 minutes. Rinse under cold running water and pat dry with absorbent kitchen paper.
2   Heat oil in a heavy-based frypan. Add eggplant and cook until lightly browned. Remove eggplant from pan and set aside.
3   Add onion to frypan and cook for 4-5 minutes or until onion softens. Add tomatoes, parsley, mint and eggplant and cook for a further 5 minutes. Stir in rice and chicken stock. Bring the boil. Reduce heat, cover and simmer for 30 minutes. Allow to stand for 30 minutes before serving.

❖

LONTONG

Lontong are traditionally wrapped in young banana leaves. If these are not readily available, you can successfully substitute aluminium foil. The fried onion flakes that we have used in this recipe can be purchased from Asian food stores.

Serves 6

- [ ] **young banana leaves or aluminium foil**
- [ ] **500 g (1 lb) shortgrain white rice, well washed**
- [ ] **2 tablespoons sweet soy sauce**
- [ ] **2 tablespoons fried onion flakes**

1   If using banana leaves, drop in boiling water to clean and soften. Remove leaves from water and pat dry with absorbent kitchen paper. Brush lightly with a little vegetable oil. Cut leaves or foil into 20 cm (8 in) squares.
2   Place a large spoonful of rice in the centre of each square and fold over to completely encase, allowing a little room for expansion during cooking. Tie each parcel with string to secure.
3   Bring a large saucepan of water to the boil, drop in rice bundles and simmer for 1 hour. To serve, drain bundles, unwrap and sprinkle with soy sauce and onion flakes.

Rice Dishes

Where would we be without rice? It is the staple diet of many millions of people and comes in all shapes, sizes and even colours! Since rice forms the authentic accompaniment to many of our dishes, rich or simple, spicy or mild, we'll show you ways you can produce perfect rice with ease – anytime. For a special treat, try sprinkling a spoonful or two of fresh parsley, thyme or oregano in cooked rice.

Left: Pilaf with Eggplant, Lontong, Rose Scented Saffron Rice

A-Z of Spices

Don't be discouraged by their unpronounceable names or by the (false) idea that they are expensive or complicated to use. Spices are the good cook's greatest asset. This chapter is devoted to demystifying cardamom and cumin, cinnamon and cloves – and that's just the C's!

Allspice. The seeds of allspice are just slightly larger than peppercorns and dark brown in colour. Allspice is a delicately spicy mingling of cloves, cinnamon and nutmeg, with cloves predominating. Allspice berries are the dried fruit of a tall, aromatic evergreen of the myrtle and clove family, which can grow to over 12 m. Picked when green and unripe, the seeds are dried in the sun to a rich, deep brown colour.

Aniseed. The small, oval grey-green ribbed seeds of anise have a warm, sweet, pungent flavour and can be used in sweet and savoury dishes. The aromatic anise annual grows to about 60 cm high and is similar to other small members of the parsley family. Anise will grow well in a good summer in light, dry loamy soil in a sunny position. Sow the seeds in mid-spring. The plants produce small white flowers and fern-like leaves.

Caraway. A handsome biennial to 60 cm high with finely cut leaves and clusters of white flowers which produce aromatic seeds with their characteristic flavour. Sow seeds direct in spring or autumn. Needs a sunny, well drained position protected from wind. Young leaves are used as a garnish for cooked vegetables. The seeds are used in dishes of cabbage, potatoes and parsnips. Also used in some cakes, biscuits and apple pie. Leaves and softer stems can be eaten in salads or cooked with other vegetables.

Cardamom. The cardamom bush is a herbaceous perennial plant of the ginger family and grows nearly 3 m high. Cardamom will only grow in a hot climate. It produces slightly pungent, highly aromatic pods holding seeds which are sweet with a camphor-like flavour.

Cassia. The bark, unripe seeds and the dried leaves of this plant are all used in cooking. Related to cinnamon, the bark can be used in the same way and has a similar taste but is not as strong. The seeds also known as Chinese cassia buds, are used in drinks and confectionery and are often added to pot pourris.

Cayenne Pepper. Cayenne pepper, paprika and Tabasco sauce are all made from varieties of capsicum. Cayenne is derived from a hot, red variety of capsicum called 'bird chilli'. Although cayenne is not as hot as some chilli powders it is very pungent and should be used sparingly. Store in an airtight container in small quantities and in a dark place.

Celery Seeds. These seeds with a bitter celery flavour, are the tiny light brown seeds of the celery plant. They should be used sparingly in casseroles and soups. They are a great addition to pickled vegetables, homemade bread and will add life to any salad dressing.

Chilli. Chillies belong to the capsicum family and have an especially hot flavour. All varieties of peppers bear certain common characteristics. The bushy chilli shrub prefers tropical or sub-tropical climates and grows to between 30 cm to 1.8. m high, depending on the variety. As a general rule, the smaller, narrower and darker the chilli, the greater its pungency; unripe fresh chillies are usually less pungent than ripe fresh ones, and these in turn are milder than dried chillies.

Cinnamon. Cinnamon is the bark of a tree which belongs to the laurel family. The cinnamon tree is a tall, thick evergreen tree which prefers tropical climates. The bark is the most important part of the tree – when ground it provides a sweet spice highly valued for both culinary and medical usage The leaves are pointed, smooth and tough and the small creamy-white flowers are followed by dark blue berries. The dried bark is sold in small quills (usually 7.5 cm-15 cm long) or as powder.

Cloves. The clove tree is an evergreen which grows abundantly near tropical sea shores. Cloves are the highly aromatic flower buds of this tree or shrub which is native to the Moluccas or Spice Islands. Nowadays cloves are mostly imported from Zanzibar and Madagascar.

Coriander. Coriander is a member of the parsley family. The plant gives off a strong odour which is replaced by a sweet orangey aroma when the seeds are dried. The round, light brown seeds are milder than many other spices and can be used in large quantities. The taste is fresh with a hint of bitterness and can be improved by gently roasting before grinding.

Cumin Seeds. Like coriander and caraway, cumin seed comes from a plant of the parsley family. Cumin is a small and delicate annual which usually grows to 25 cm in height. Native to the Middle East, cumin now grows in most hot climates. The small, dark brown, elongated seeds have a rich sweet aroma; their flavour is similarly pungent and they should be used sparingly. Cumin seed is often confused with fennel or anise (both sometimes called 'sweet cumin').

Dill Seeds. The dill plant is another member of the parsley family and the leaves, stalks as well as the dried seeds can all be used in cooking. The oval, flattened seeds have a fresh, sweet aroma with a slightly bitter taste similar to caraway seeds. They are dried and used whole or slightly crushed. Add them to dishes towards the end of cooking or when cooking is over to fully enhance their flavour.

Fennel Seeds. Another member of the wonderful parsley family, fennel seeds are like plumper, larger versions of anise seeds with a warm and slightly bitter anise flavour. They are curved, ridged and dullish yellow-green in appearance. Fennel seeds have strong digestive qualities and so are often used with rich meats and oily fish.

Fenugreek. The fenugreek plant which grows to 30-60 cm, is a member of the bean and pea family. Its flowers and pods resemble those of the pea. Each long, narrow pod contains ten to twenty small, hard yellow-brown seeds. The seeds have a slightly bitter-sweet taste and should be used in moderation. Only when roasted do the seeds give off their pungent aroma. Whole or ground fenugreek is most often used in Indian curries.

Ginger. Ginger is an important spice in both East and West. Like other tropical plants of the same family, such as turmeric, it is the knobbly root of the ginger plant which is used as a spice. Fresh ginger does not keep well, so buy only in small quantities. Dried ginger root can be bruised and ground to a powder (its fibres removed) and used as ground ginger, or bruised and infused in the cooking liquid of savoury dishes.

Juniper Berries. The juniper tree is a small coniferous and prickly evergreen which ranges in height from 1.2-10.5 m. The round, purple-brown berries are about twice the size of peppercorns with smooth skins. The spicy pine aroma and sweet, resinous flavour varies according to where they are grown. The berries are bought whole and are easy to grind because they are soft. Juniper is commonly used in spice mixtures for meat and are excellent with pork and game.

Laos Powder. Laos powder also known as galangal or galingale, has a peppery ginger taste and is used in the hot and spicy dishes of Southeast Asia. Closely related to ginger it is similar in that it is the root of the plant that is powdered. In Europe it is used to flavour liqueurs and bitters.

Mace. Mace and nutmeg are both parts of the fruit of a tropical evergreen tree. Mace blades form the outer casing of the nutmeg and are bright red when harvested, drying to a deep orange. The flavour of mace is similar to nutmeg but more delicate.

Mustard Seeds. Mustard is internationally famous as a condiment and flavouring. The whole seeds are the basis for prepared mustards, and the pungent oil extracted from the seeds and the seeds themselves are also popularly used as culinary spices. There are three main varieties of mustard: black, brown and white. The three plants are very similar in appearance and grow to about 75-105 cm. All bear tiny, spherical, hard seeds. Brown mustard seeds are most commonly used as an Indian cooking spice.

Nutmeg. The small, oval shiny nut, about 4 cm long, is dried in its seedcoat which is then removed. Nutmeg is slightly milder than mace but has a more nutty flavour – warm and sweetish with a light bitter undertone. Nutmegs can be bought whole or ready-ground. It is best to buy them whole and store in an airtight container. Finely grate as needed.

Paprika. Like cayenne pepper, paprika is a finely ground powder made from the fruit of several different chilli plants. The ripe flesh is used for mild, sweet paprika, the seeds are included for more pungent versions. Mild paprika has a light, sweet smell and almost no pungency; the strongest paprika is similar to cayenne pepper.

Pepper. Pepper comes from the tropical trailing vine of the Piperaceae family. The vines grow to heights of 3.6 m and bear long strings of 20-30 small berries which ripen from green to reddish-yellow. Black pepper berries are picked when green and dried whole; for white pepper they are allowed to ripen and turn red and the skin is removed before drying. Green peppercorns are picked when still green and usually pickled.

Poppy Seeds. Poppy seeds, sometimes called maw seeds, come from the opium poppy. The plant is related to both the common field poppy and garden varieties. It grows to anything from 30-120 cm and bears white, pink or lilac flowers and erect oval seedpods. The tiny, hard seeds are very mild and sweetish and acquire a bitter-sweet nutty flavour when cooked.

Saffron. Saffron is the most expensive spice in the world. It is the dried stigmas of the flowers of the saffron crocus. The flowers are extracted from the freshly harvested flowers and dried to become irregular, orange-red threads about 4 cm long. It takes about 50,000 stigmas to make up 100 g of saffron! Saffron imparts a distinctive aroma, a bitter honey-like taste and a strong yellow colour to food. It's better to buy the threads and store in an airtight container in a dark place. Ground saffron can vary enormously in quality.

Sesame Seeds. Sesame is a tropical annual with a pungent smell. The plant grows to anything between 60-180 cm. The seedpods contain a large number of small, flat oval seeds in a variety of colours. They may be red, light brown or black and have a rich nutty flavour. Dry roast before use or fry lightly until they just colour and give off a roasted aroma.

Star Anise. Star anise is the star-shaped fruit of an oriental evergreen of the magnolia family which can reach a height of 7.3 m. When dried it is a brown colour and the flavour is one of pungent aniseed. Whole stars store well in an airtight container, and are preferable to the powdered form.

Tamarind. Tamarind with its sour flavour is a large pod that grows on the Indian tamarind tree. It is picked, seeded and peeled before being pressed into a dark brown pulp. Tamarind is usually mixed with warm water to give tamarind juice which is then used in chutneys, sauces and curries.

Turmeric. Turmeric is a typical member of the ginger family, and like ginger it is the knobbly roots or rhizomes which form the cooking spice. The tropical turmeric has spiky yellow flowers and long, shiny pointed leaves, and can grow to a height of 1 m. Turmeric has a strong woody aroma and distinctive, pungent flavour. Because of this it should not be used as a cheap substitute for saffron.

Vanilla. The dark brown pod of vanilla comes from a type of orchid native to South America. It was discovered by the Spaniards in Mexico. When first picked the pod is a yellow green and it is only after curing and drying that it becomes the dark brown we associate with vanilla. Essentially a flavouring used in sweet dishes such as ice cream, custards and rice, it is also popular as a flavouring for wine cups, hot chocolate and coffee drinks. The vanilla pod can be used several times and if kept in a jar of sugar will flavour it to make vanilla sugar.

SPICE ADVICE

✦ The best tasting spices are those that are freshly ground. Peppercorns, allspice and nutmeg can have their own mills. A pestle and mortar is ideal for crushing small amounts of spice, while larger quantities can be ground in a coffee grinder - kept for this purpose. Do not grind spices in the same grinder as you use for coffee as the flavours mix and the result is spiced coffee or coffee flavoured spices.

✦ When handling fresh chillies do not put your hands near your eyes or allow them to touch your lips. To avoid discomfort and burning, wear rubber gloves. Freshly minced chilli is also available in jars from supermarkets.

✦ To store fresh ginger, peel and place in a glass jar. Cover with sherry or green ginger wine, store in the refrigerator and use as you would fresh ginger. Ginger will keep in this way for many months. The sherry or wine left after the ginger is used is ideal to use in cooking or dressings.

✦ Yoghurt is a natural cooler, in Indian and Middle Eastern cooking it is used to offset the hotness of chillies and rawness of spices. It can be combined with other ingredients or served as a side dish so that people can help themselves when they feel that the palate needs cooling. The Indians drink a yoghurt drink called lassi when eating curry, to counteract the heat of the food, refresh the palate and aid digestion.

✦ Stem ginger also known as preserved or Chinese ginger, is the tender young roots which have been cleaned and peeled then simmered in a syrup. It is often sold in pretty Chinese jars and given as gifts at Christmas.

✦ A delicious and easy way to add taste to cabbage or spinach is to toss with a pinch of nutmeg and a knob of butter.

AT A GLANCE SPICE GUIDE

A guide to using spices

SPICE	SOUPS	MAIN DISHES
Allspice	beef and minestrone soups	baked ham, meat loaf, spiced meats
Aniseed	cream soups	seafood, pork and poultry dishes
Cardamom	spiced and curried soups	curries and spicy dishes of Indian and Middle Eastern origin
Cassia		Chinese dishes and curries
Cayenne Pepper	soups, especially fish and tomato	curries and spicy dishes, egg dishes
Chilli – fresh	spicy soups	all curries and spicy meat, poultry, fish and egg dishes
Chilli – powder	spicy soups	as for fresh chillies
Coriander – seed	spicy soups	curries and spicy meat, poultry, fish
Cumin – seed	spicy soups	meat, poultry and fish dishes
Curry Plant	fish and spicy soups	casseroles and curries
Dill – seed	vegetable soups	lamb, pork and fish dishes
Fennel – seed		chicken and fish dishes
Fenugreek		Indian and Middle Eastern Dishes
Ginger – fresh		curries
Ginger – ground		curries, baked ham and fish dishes
Mace		fish, chicken, beef and veal dishes
Mustard – powder	leek and celery soups	grilled meats, ham casseroles
Mustard – seed		curries, pork, rabbit , veal, some fish dishes
Nutmeg	cream soups	fish, chicken, egg and cheese dishes, pasta
Paprika	most soups	curries, goulashes, pork, beef, veal and fish dishes
Saffron	especially fish soups	chicken, fish, turkey and some egg dishes, paella
Turmeric	curried and spicy soups	curries, egg and fish dishes
Vanilla		

VEGETABLE DISHES	DESSERTS AND BAKED PRODUCTS	OTHER USES
carrot, pea and potato salads	apple desserts such as pies and crumbles, milk puddings	pickles, confectionery, stewed fruit
salads, carrots and zucchini	biscuits, cakes, fresh fruit, especially good with figs	cheese dips
vegetable curries	bread and yeast cakes, custards, fruit salads	pickles, stewed fruit, savoury and sweet rice dishes
ground sprinkle over vegetables		poached and stewed fruit
		salad dressings
spicy vegetable dishes		salad dressings
spicy vegetable dishes		salad dressings, dips, pickles, sauces
spicy vegetable dishes	biscuits, cakes, fruit salad	yoghurt dips, salad dressings, stewed fruit
cabbage, carrots and legume dishes		pickles, chutneys, marinades, rice dishes
		stuffings for veal and game
cucumber, marrow, cabbage and carrots	biscuits, cakes, fruit salad	pickles
potatoes	biscuits, sprinkle over breads and buns	salad dressings, sauces for fish
sprouts used in salads		
	biscuits, cakes and cooked apple dishes	marinades
vegetable curries and spicy legume dishes	cakes, biscuits, puddings, fruit pies	pickles, spiced drinks such as mulled wine, stewed fruit
	biscuits, cakes	flavour whipped cream, stuffings, pate
braised celery and leeks		salad dressings, stuffings
cabbage and celery		stuffings
cabbage, carrots and root vegetables	biscuits, cakes, milk puddings, pastries, fruit salads, junket, sweet breads	stewed fruits, flavour, whipped cream, pates
legume dishes		rice dishes
	biscuits, cakes, bread	savoury rice dishes
	colouring for cakes and breads	rice dishes
	custards, ice cream, milk puddings	flavour cream, drinks, sugar and cups

Herbs, Spices and All That's Nice

The secret of many heart warming dishes is a combination of herbs or spices. Many of these are available ready made, but nothing can compare with the fresh taste of homemade curry powder or a freshly picked and assembled bouquet garni. This section tells you the secrets of garam masala, five spice powder and many other delicious combinations.

❖

FINES HERBS

Fines herbs is a mixture of fresh chopped herbs used to flavour sauces, cream cheeses, meat dishes, sauteed vegetables and omelettes. The following is the traditional combination, but you can vary it depending on what you wish to flavour.

- ☐ **30 g (1 oz) chopped fresh parsley**
- ☐ **15 g (¹/₂ oz) chopped fresh chervil**
- ☐ **15 g (¹/₂ oz) chopped fresh chives**
- ☐ **30 g (1 oz) chopped fresh tarragon**

Combine parsley, chervil, chives and tarragon and use as required.

❖

BOUQUET GARNI

A bouquet garni is the French term for a small bunch of herbs and spices which is used to add flavour to a dish, in particular casseroles and soups. Bouquet garni is available ready-made, however, it is easy to make and the flavour is superior. Use the following recipe to make a basic bouquet garni and try some of the other variations for a change.

- ☐ **2 sprigs fresh parsley**
- ☐ **2 sprigs fresh thyme**
- ☐ **1 fresh or dried bay leaf**

Place herb stems together and tie with string.

VARIATIONS

✦ If using dried herbs, place 1 teaspoon dried parsley, ¹/₂ teaspoon dried thyme and a small crumbled bay leaf on a piece of muslin, bring the corners together and tie with a piece of string.
When making chicken stock, use lemon thyme in place of thyme and tie a strip of lemon rind into the bouquet garni.
✦ When making beef stock, tie a strip of orange rind and a few celery leaves into the bouquet garni.

❖

GARAM MASALA

Garam masala is a popular mixture of ground spices used extensively in Indian cooking. It is available ready-made but if you cannot get it, you can easily make it yourself. Just vary the amounts of the ingredients according to personal taste.

- ☐ **2 cardamom pods, husks removed**
- ☐ **2 teaspoons cumin seeds**
- ☐ **2 teaspoons coriander seeds**
- ☐ **1 teaspoon black peppercorns**
- ☐ **1 teaspoon whole cloves**
- ☐ **1 cinnamon stick**
- ☐ **¹/₂ nutmeg, grated**

1 Heat a heavy-based frypan over a medium heat. Add cardamom seeds, cumin seeds, coriander seeds, peppercorns, cloves, and cinnamon stick. Stir constantly until evenly browned.
2 Remove spices from the pan and allow to cool.
3 Grind roasted spices and nutmeg to make a fine powder.

❖

FIVE SPICE POWDER

Five Spice Powder, a favourite ingredient in Chinese cooking, adds a subtle anise flavour to Oriental dishes. The Chinese make their own mixtures and no two recipes are ever the same. Making your own Five Spice Powder allows you to alter the ingredients to suit your personal taste.

- ☐ **2 teaspoons anise pepper**
- ☐ **2 teaspoons star anise**
- ☐ **1 cinnamon stick**
- ☐ **2 teaspoons whole cloves**
- ☐ **2 teaspoons fennel seeds**

Place anise pepper, star anise, cinnamon, cloves and fennel seeds in a blender or coffee grinder and grind to a fine powder. Store in an airtight container.

CURRY POWDER

Curry powder can be purchased in any supermarket, however, making your own is easy and adds a very special taste to any dish. This curry powder will keep in an airtight container for up to 3 months.

- [ ] **1 tablespoon cumin seeds**
- [ ] **1 tablespoon fenugreek seeds**
- [ ] **1 teaspoon mustard seeds**
- [ ] **1 tablespoon black peppercorns**
- [ ] **4 tablespoons coriander seeds**
- [ ] **2 teaspoons ground ginger**
- [ ] **$^1/_2$ teaspoon chilli powder**
- [ ] **2 tablespoons ground turmeric**

Place cumin seeds, fenugreek seeds, mustard seeds, peppercorns, coriander seeds, ginger, chilli powder and turmeric in a blender or coffee grinder and grind to a fine powder. Store in an airtight container.

CURRY PASTES

Curry pastes are available from Oriental and Asian supermarkets. However they are easy to make yourself, if they are not available locally. It is best to make these pastes in fairly small quantities as generally only a small amount is required in a recipe and most of the home-made pastes only keep for a month or so.

MASALA CURRY PASTE

- [ ] **3 tablespoons grated fresh ginger**
- [ ] **1 teaspoon ground turmeric**
- [ ] **1 teaspoon ground cloves**
- [ ] **2 cloves garlic, crushed**
- [ ] **60 g (2 oz) fresh coriander leaves**
- [ ] **60 g (2 oz) fresh mint leaves**
- [ ] **1 teaspoon ground cardamom**
- [ ] **125 mL (4 fl.oz) cider vinegar**
- [ ] **60 mL (2 fl.oz) peanut oil**
- [ ] **2 teaspoons sesame oil**

1   Place ginger, turmeric, cloves, garlic, coriander, mint, cardamom and vinegar in a food processor or blender and process until well combined.
2   Heat peanut and sesame oils in a small saucepan, stir in spice mixture. Bring to the boil, remove from heat and allow to cool.

RED HOT CURRY PASTE

- [ ] **4 dried red chillies, seeded and chopped**
- [ ] **1 large onion, chopped**
- [ ] **2 cloves garlic, crushed**
- [ ] **1 tablespoon peanut oil**
- [ ] **1 teaspoon lemon juice**
- [ ] **2 teaspoons ground cumin**
- [ ] **2 teaspoons paprika**
- [ ] **1 teaspoon ground turmeric**
- [ ] **1 teaspoon ground black pepper**

Place chillies, onion, garlic, oil, lemon juice, cumin, paprika, turmeric and pepper in a food processor or blender and process until well combined.

HOMEMADE YOGHURT

Even though yoghurt takes a little time to make, there is not a great deal of work involved. The following recipe is a simple method for making yoghurt. The commercial yoghurt will only be required the first time you make it, after that you can keep some of the yoghurt from the first batch to use in the next.

- [ ] **600 mL (1 pt) milk**
- [ ] **1 tablespoon commercial yoghurt**

Bring milk to the boil, then allow to cool to lukewarm. When lukewarm stir in yoghurt. Stir well and place in a thermos for 10–12 hours, alternatively the yoghurt can be kept in a warm place.

PARSLEY BUTTER

- [ ] **125 g (4 oz) butter**
- [ ] **2 tablespoons finely chopped parsley**
- [ ] **squeeze lemon juice**
- [ ] **pinch cayenne pepper**

1   Cream butter then beat in parsley, lemon juice and cayenne.
2   Shape butter into a roll and wrap in greaseproof paper. Place in refrigerator and allow to harden.

FLAVOURED BUTTER

The most popular flavoured butter is garlic butter, but many other flavoured butters are just as easy to make and as delicious. Use flavoured butters not only for garlic or herb breads, but also to toss through steamed vegetables or to spread on bread or canapes. They are also delicious cut into slices and used to top grilled meats or fish.

CHILLI BUTTER

- [ ] **125 g (4 oz) butter**
- [ ] **$^1/_4$ teaspoon chilli powder, or according to taste**
- [ ] **squeeze lemon juice**

1   Cream butter, then beat in chilli powder and lemon juice.
2   Shape butter into a roll and wrap in greaseproof paper. Place in refrigerator and allow to harden.

GHEE

Ghee is a form of clarified butter used extensively in Asian cooking. It is very easy to make and keeps almost indefinitely in the refrigerator.

- [ ] **250 g (8 oz) butter**

1   Melt butter in a heavy-based saucepan over medium heat. Continue to heat until a thick froth forms on the surface.
2   Reduce heat and simmer until froth starts to separate from the clear butter and the sediment starts to settle on the bottom of the pan. Heat for 1 minute more, remove pan from heat and allow butter to cool slightly.
3   Line a metal sieve with muslin or a double thickness of kitchen paper and strain the butter into a glass storage jar. Discard sediment left in the bottom of the pan. Allow ghee to cool and set and cover tightly with plastic food wrap.

A-Z of Herbs

Few ingredients are as tasty as fresh herbs, plucked from a window box or from a special section of your garden. Many grow with just the slightest encouragement, while others need attention, but either way you'll be amply repaid in flavoursome meals. Here we look at the major herbs and their culinary uses.

Angelica. This is a stout biennial or perennial herb which grows to 2 m or more. Leaves are soft green and divided into large leaflets. The stems are round, ribbed and hollow with yellow-green flowers which grow in a ball-like cluster. Best suited to cool-climate areas where it can be planted in sun or semi-shade. Shelter from strong wind is desirable because the stems are brittle. Angelica is completely permeated by a unique essence, giving it a delicately sweet and refreshing aroma. Angelica stems can be candied, and can also be used instead of sugar when stewing sour fruits like rhubarb. The roots are edible and can be served as a vegetable. The seeds are used in flavouring gin and some liqueurs.

Basil. An annual to 60 cm high with peppery, clove-scented leaves. There are different types of basil plants but the old favourites sweet basil and bush basil are still the best varieties to grow for the kitchen. Grow from seed in a sunny, moist but well-drained position sheltered from wind. For the best results, sow the seed at the end of spring or at the beginning of summer. Remove the small, white, lipped flower buds to encourage longer life. For a stronger flavour in cooking, use fresh basil leaves as basil loses a lot of its flavour when dried. Excellent with all tomato dishes and torn up in salads. It goes well with carrots, zucchini, pasta sauces and chicken.

Bay. A slow-growing evergreen tree with aromatic leaves, also known as bay laurel or sweet bay. Bay trees make excellent tub specimens and should be grown in a sunny sheltered position. Young plants need protection from frosts. The leaves are large, flat, oval and glossy and can be harvested at any time of the year. Bay leaves have a strong flavour and taste rather bitter when fresh so are most often used dried. A bay leaf is one of the three herbs that make up the classic bouquet garni. Use with tomatoes and beetroot and to flavour soups, sauces and stews. Add bay leaves to stores of flour, pulses and similar foods to keep weevils away.

Borage. This herb is an annual with thick, soft stems, large leaves and branching hairy stems. Height varies from 30-90 cm. Leaves are greyish-green, about 10-15 cm long. Star-like summer flowers in white or blue are most attractive. Flowering can continue through winter in mild areas. Flowers and young leaves can be eaten. The leaves have a delicate, cucumber-like flavour. Finely chop and use as a garnish in salads. The flowers can be candied. Both flowers and leaves can be dipped in a light batter and deep-fried.

Chervil. A small spreading annual to 50 cm. Fern-like leaves have a delicate aniseed flavour. The white flowers, which appear in early summer, grow in small, flat umbels. The seeds which follow resemble caraway seeds but are longer and thinner. The seeds should be sown in shallow drills 30 cm apart in spring and autumn. Grow in a partially shaded, sheltered position in rich, moist soil. Keep chervil watered at all times Chervil leaves are delicious with salad greens and spinach. Use in dressings, garnish for soups, and with fish dishes.

Chives. A perennial member of the onion family, chives have hollow onion-flavoured leaves and attractive edible mauve flowers. Chives like a rich, moist soil in full sun; they also grow well indoors in pots on a sunny window sill. They respond to picking in moderation, but a proportion of fresh leaves must be left. In cold climates, chives die back in winter. Chives should be lifted and divided every two or three years in spring or autumn, or immediately after flowering. Use in fresh salads and to flavour potatoes or any of the marrow family. Good in most savoury dishes and excellent with eggs and cream.

Coriander. Sometimes called Chinese parsley or cilantro, coriander is an attractive annual to 60 cm. The lacy foliage has a distinctive, strong aroma quite different from other similar herbs such as anise, caraway, dill and fennel, all of whose leaves have a warm spicy anise-scent. A mixture of lemon peel and sage is one description of the flavour of fresh coriander leaves. Coriander can be grown either in a sunny spot in the garden or indoors in pots on a sunny window sill, by planting the whole coriander seeds. Sow seeds direct in

spring and water generously. Harvest seeds in autumn and dry in a light, airy position. When the small oval coriander seeds have hardened and ripened to a pale fawn colour, they are one of the most deliciously fragrant of all spices used in cooking. Coriander is used in almost every Thai dish. Leaves are tasty in salads and as a garnish for pea soup. The seeds complement mushrooms, cauliflower, beetroot and celery and are commonly used in curries, sausage-making and as a flavouring in cakes.

Curry Plant. The curry plant is a shrubby perennial plant that grows into a low spreading bush with silvery-grey, green spiky leaves. Although it is not used in authentic curries, the leaves do have a strong curry-like flavour.

Curry Leaves. Not to be confused with the silvery-grey leaves of the curry plant. Curry leaves are small, shiny and evergreen and slightly like small bay leaves. The tree is easily grown and decorative, with an exotic spicy fragrance. Curry leaves are usually chopped and fried in oil at the start of making curry. They quickly turn brown and become crisp when the other ingredients are added. The leaves may also be ground to a powder and used in making curry powder and paste.

Dill. A fast-growing, upright annual to 90 cm, dill resembles fennel in that both have hollow stems, feathery leaves and clusters of yellow flowers. The flavour of dill is clean and delicate. Sow seeds in a sunny, well-drained soil in spring and autumn. The seeds can be harvested. Dill grows best in a light, medium-rich soil with plenty of moisture. Dill seeds and leaves can both be eaten. Dill seed flavours and helps the digestion of steamed cabbage, coleslaw, sauerkraut, cucumbers, various chutneys and pickles, pastries, breads, sauces and cooked root vegetables. Both the seeds and leaves with their spicy flavour are used, although the foliage does not have the same concentration of oil as the seeds.

Fennel. Fast-growing tall annual to 1.5 m. It has bright green, feathery leaves and clusters of yellow flowers followed by aniseed-flavoured seeds. Grow in a well-drained, sunny position and provide plenty of water. Both leaves and seeds are traditionally used with fish. If baking a whole fish branches of the foliage make a fragrant bed for the fish to rest on during cooking. Fennel seeds are used in soups, sauces and with lentils, rice and potatoes. Also used in breads and cakes. The leaves are used in salads, relishes and as garnishes.

Garlic. A bulbous perennial plant with strap-like leaves measuring approximately 25 mm across and 30 cm long. A willowy, round flower-stalk thrusts upwards above the leaves, and the flower that appears is a compact collection of mauve-tinted white petals. Plant separated cloves in early spring in a rich and well-drained soil, preferably in full sun. When the foliage has died down at the end of summer, the bulbs can be carefully lifted. Dig the bulbs, shake them free of dirt and plait several together. Hang the plaited garlic in a dry, well-ventilated place. The whole garlic plant has a pungent, lingering odour – it cannot be called scent or aroma due to the essential oil it contains. The oil is antibiotic and contains Vitamins A and B, sulphur and iodine.

G *inger.* A tall perennial plant to 1.5 m high with spikes of white and purple flowers and aromatic rhizomes, ginger prefers a hot, humid climate in a rich, well-drained soil in partial shade. Ginger root has a sweet, hot flavour which goes with meat, fish, vegetables, cakes and sweets. Fresh grated ginger is particularly good with steamed or stir-fried vegetables, especially Chinese cabbage. Ginger is an essential part of many curries, pickles and chutneys.

H *orseradish.* A hardy perennial with long, elliptical dark green leaves. It grows to a height of about 60 cm with erect stems and has small, scented, four-petalled white flowers. Often grown for its thick, fleshy, aromatic roots – hot, pungent and full of flavour. Plant in an open sunny position, with a deeply dug, fertile soil. Horseradish sauce uses grated roots mixed with cream or some similar viscous liquid. It must be used raw as the cooked roots lose

their flavour. Roots can be grated and dried and stored in airtight containers for later use. The leaves are also pungent and tasty and can be chopped and used as a salad ingredient.

L *emon Balm.* A perennial to 90 cm, lemon balm has dark green, heart-shaped leaves that have a strong lemon scent and flavour. Grow in a rich, well-drained soil in full sun. Pinch back in early summer to encourage new growth. Use only fresh leaves sprinkled over vegetable or fruit salads. Use leaves in fish and poultry dishes, sauces, marinades and stuffings. Lemon balm is sometimes planted in orchards to attract bees to pollinate the fruit blossom.

L *emon Grass.* A grass-like perennial to 3 m high, lemon grass has pointed aromatic leaves with a delicious lemon scent. It forms a large clump in a sunny, warm position with plenty of water, but needs good drainage. The fleshy white lower part of the leaves is used in South-East Asian dishes. It adds a tangy taste to salads and is a must for curries.

M *arjoram.* A fragrant perennial plant to 75 cm high with small oval leaves and clusters of white or mauve flowers. Grow in full sun in a well-drained soil and keep trimmed to encourage fresh, compact growth. Fresh leaves are used in tomato dishes, with any of the cabbage family and green beans. Marjoram is an excellent addition to spicy meat dishes. It can be included in meat sauces for pasta, meatloafs and rice stuffings for vegetables.

M *int.* There are many varieties of mint, but spearmint (Mentha spicata) and applemint (Mentha suaveolens) are the two most commonly used in cooking. They are fast-growing perennials which prefer a rich, moist soil and light shade. Freshly chopped and used with peas, new potatoes, zucchini and mixed green salad. Also good in fruit salads, cooling drinks, jellies, vinegar and lamb sauce.

O *regano.* A small spreading perennial to around 50 cm. Small, pungent leaves and tiny white or mauve flowers. Grow in a well-drained soil in a sunny position. The common confusion between marjoram and oregano can be resolved by realising that the cultivated marjoram comes from the wild oregano and that the first has a sweet flavour and the second a strong, peppery one. Fresh marjoram leaves are used to season salads and many tomato dishes, especially tomato sauces used with pasta. It is also used with eggplant, beans, zucchini and cheese.

Parsley. A biennial plant to 60 cm high with flat or curly leaves. Parsley is grown from seed which should be sown direct in spring and summer. Parsley likes a rich, well-drained soil in partial or full sun, and responds to frequent feeding. It is one of the best herbs of all and can be added to soups, stews, casseroles, sauces and stuffings. Always include the chopped stems as they are full of flavour and nutriment.

Rosemary. A Mediterranean evergreen shrub to around 1.6 m high. It has thin, dark-green leaves, silver on the underside, highly aromatic; the pale blue flowers grow along the stems as well as at the tips. Choose a sheltered, sunny spot for planting, preferably against a wall, or in a corner, as rosemary needs all the protection it can get. The leaves, used either fresh or dried, are good with meat dishes, particularly lamb. The flavour is strong so they should be used sparingly.

Sage. A small perennial shrub with soft, grey-green leaves and blue flowers during summer. Grow in a sunny, well-drained position and trim regularly. Give it plenty of water during summer. The leaves, used either fresh or dried, have a strong, clean flavour which cuts the grease of fatty foods. Use chopped fresh leaves sparingly in salads, potato dishes and with cheese. Use with pork and veal and in seasoning.

Savory, Summer. An annual to 60 cm high with tender, narrow leaves of brownish-green and tiny flowers from pink to lavender. Grow in a sunny, well-drained position with plenty of organic matter added. Summer savory grows easily from seed in both warm and temperate climates. It is traditionally served with broad beans, cooked green beans and green bean salad. Also good in stuffings, rice, soups, sauces and stews.

Savory, Winter. A semi-prostrate perennial with narrow green leaves and pale blue flowers. Likes full sun and a well-drained soil with plenty of organic matter added. Particularly good used in stuffings, rice, soups, sauces and stews.

Sorrel. A perennial to 90 cm tall with large bright green, arrow-shaped leaves that have a sharp lemony, bitter taste. Sorrel prefers a well-drained, rich soil in sun or semi-shade. Young fresh leaves are excellent in a mixed green salad. A few leaves can be added when cooking spinach. Used in the classic French sorrel soup. Use also in sauces and vegetable purees.

Tarragon. French tarragon is a bushy perennial to around 1 m high. It has dark slender leaves with a slight anise flavour. Grow in a moderately rich, well-drained soil in a sunny spot. French tarragon can only be propagated by division. Use with fish, shellfish, poultry, game, veal, liver, kidneys and in egg dishes. Tarragon vinegar is an essential ingredient in Bearnaise sauce.

Thyme. A strongly aromatic shrubby perennial to around 45 cm high. It has tiny, oval leaves and bears pretty pastel-coloured flowers. There are many varieties including lemon thyme, caraway thyme and a pretty variegated type. All thymes like a sunny position with a light, well-drained soil. Trim to keep compact. Thyme is one of the most successful herbs for drying. Use fresh leaves sparingly with most vegetables including beetroot, tomatoes and zucchini. Use in casseroles, meat dishes, pates and stuffings.

AT A GLANCE HERB GUIDE

A guide to using herbs

HERB	SOUPS	MAIN DISHES
Angelica		
Basil	tomato and fish soups	fish dishes, meat loaf, casseroles
Bay	all soups and stocks	meat, fish and poultry dishes
Caraway	vegetable soups	veal and pork dishes
Chervil	fish and vegetable soups	chicken, egg, cheese dishes, casseroles
Chives	chilled soups, vichysoisse	egg dishes, meat and chicken dishes
Coriander – fresh	chilled soups	Oriental and Middle Eastern cooking, seafood, poultry, meat dishes
Curry plant	fish and spiced soups	seafood, all curries, casseroles and stews
Dill – fresh	fish and vegetable soups	fish, lamb and pork dishes
Fennel – fresh	fish and vegetable soups	chicken, fish, pork and egg dishes
Marjoram	vegetable and meat soups	casseroles, meat, marinades, meat loaf
Mint	summer soups	lamb dishes, trout
Oregano	minestrone and tomato soups	Italian dishes, pasta and egg dishes, quiches, pizza
Parsley	all soups	all fish, poultry, meat and egg dishes, pasta
Rosemary	meat stocks, chicken and tomato soups	lamb and chicken dishes
Sage	minestrone, chicken, tomato, celery and lentil soups	meat loaf, pork, cheese and egg dishes
Savory	vegetable soups	beef, pork, egg and cheese dishes, pork pies, sausages, dishes made using pulses
Sorrel	sorrel and vegetable soups	omelettes, chicken and veal dishes
Tarragon	fish and tomato soups	fish, chicken and some egg dishes
Thyme	vegetable and meat soups and stocks	meat, chicken and pasta dishes

VEGETABLE DISHES	DESSERTS AND BAKED PRODUCTS	OTHER USES
	stems are candied and used for decoration, cook with fruit	
tomato and green salads, baked vegetables dishes		dips, savouries, herb sandwiches, pasta sauces, stuffings
vegetable casseroles	place a leaf on a baked rice pudding or a baked custard	flavour pates and terrines
vegetable dishes, especially good with cabbage dishes, coleslaw and salads	biscuits, breads, cakes, pastries	stewed fruit
salads, root vegetable dishes	savoury breads and biscuits	herb butters, meat sauces
salads, potato dishes		dips, herb butters, garnish
green salads, oriental dishes		dips, pickles
		stuffings for veal and game
especially good with cucumber and cauliflower		fish sauces, cheese dips
salads		stuffings, salad dressings
tomato dishes, potato and vegetable casseroles	herb scones	sauces, herb butters, stuffings
new potatoes, peas, carrots, salads	fruit salads, ice cream	summer drinks, mint sauce, stuffings
onions, potatoes, capsicums	herb bread	pates, stuffings
all vegetables and salads	herb and savoury bread	dressings, stuffings, garnish for most savoury dishes
eggplant, tomatoes, cabbage	herb and savoury breads and scones	dressings, stuffings, dumplings, pates
salads, vegetarian casseroles	savoury breads and scones	herbal teas
broad and green beans		stuffings for pork and veal
spinach		stuffings for veal, chicken and lamb
mushrooms, carrots, salads		sauces, stuffings and dressings
most vegetable dishes		sauces, stuffings, herbal teas

Chutneys and Pickles

Sweet mango chutney, pungent pickled radish, preserved limes – they all add that "je ne sais quoi" to the recipes in this book. Yes, you can buy chutneys and pickles, but making them yourself allows you to control the sweetness, the fire or the tartness of the end result.

Pickled Ginger, Pickled Vegetable Medley, Preserved Limes

❖

PICKLED GINGER

This Chinese version of pickled ginger will keep well stored in the refrigerator.

Makes 750 mL (1 ¼ pts)

- ☐ **500 g (1 lb) fresh ginger, peeled and thinly sliced**
- ☐ **1 tablespoon salt**
- ☐ **1 L (1 ¾ pts) boiling water**
- ☐ **2 fresh chillies, seeds removed and sliced**
- ☐ **375 mL (12 fl. oz) white vinegar**
- ☐ **75 g (2 ½ oz) sugar**

1   Rub ginger slices with half the salt. Set aside and allow to stand for 10–15 minutes.
2   Pour boiling water over ginger to cover and allow to stand for 3 minutes. Drain and repeat with remaining boiling water. Drain ginger and pat dry, set aside to cool.
3   Place chillies, vinegar and sugar in a saucepan. Bring to the boil and cook until sugar dissolves. Remove from heat and set aside to cool.
4   Pack ginger into sterilised jars and pour over vinegar mixture. Mix using a pair of chopsticks. Seal and label. Store in the refrigerator until required.

❖

PICKLED VEGETABLE MEDLEY

This colourful pickle looks very attractive if vegetables are packed into the jars in layers. The pickle originated in the Middle East but is delicious served with any meat or poultry dish.

Makes 2 litres (3 ½ pts)

- ☐ **½ cauliflower, cut into florets**
- ☐ **1 green capsicum, cut into strips**
- ☐ **1 red capsicum, cut into strips**
- ☐ **2 green tomatoes, sliced**
- ☐ **2 carrots, peeled and sliced**
- ☐ **2 stalks celery, sliced**
- ☐ **75 g (2 ½ oz) salt**
- ☐ **1 L (1 ¾ pts) water**
- ☐ **250 mL (8 fl. oz) white vinegar**
- ☐ **1 tablespoon sugar**
- ☐ **2 red chillies**
- ☐ **sprigs fresh dill**
- ☐ **2 cloves garlic, peeled**

1   Layer vegetables in a baking dish and sprinkle each layer with a little salt. Set aside to stand for 6 hours. Rinse and drain.
2   Place water, vinegar, sugar and remaining salt in a saucepan. Bring to the boil, stirring until sugar and salt are dissolved. Set aside and allow to cool.
3   Pack layered vegetables into warm sterilised jars. Place whole chillies, dill sprigs and garlic cloves in jars to give an attractive appearance. Pour over the cold brine. Seal and label. Allow to stand for 1 week before using.

❖

PRESERVED LIMES

Nothing is more refreshing than the tart taste of the lime. This recipe will ensure that you have these small precious fruits to enjoy at any time of the year. The limes are ready when the skins are soft and juice has thickened.

Makes 2 litres (3 ½ pts)

- ☐ **25 fresh limes**
- ☐ **12 small red chillies**
- ☐ **3 large green chillies, sliced**
- ☐ **2 cm piece ginger, cut into strips**
- ☐ **2 tablespoons black mustard seeds**
- ☐ **2 tablespoons fenugreek seeds**
- ☐ **4 bay leaves**
- ☐ **2 tablespoons sugar**
- ☐ **2 tablespoons salt**

1   Cut 8 of the limes into quarters. Squeeze the juice from the remaining limes and reserve.
2   Layer limes in a sterilised glass jar. Place red chillies, green chilli slices, ginger, a sprinkling of mustard and fenugreek seeds, a bay leaf and a pinch of sugar and salt between each layer. Cover with lime juice and place muslin cloth over the jar.
3   Stand jar in a warm place and add a pinch of sugar and salt every day for four days. Seal and store for 6 weeks before using.

USING PRESERVED LIMES

Lemons can also be preserved in this way. Preserved limes and lemons are an essential part of Mediterranean cookery. Usually only the peel and the juice are used in the wonderfully aromatic stews and casseroles of this area. The fruit imparts a unique flavour to these dishes. A white film will often form on the preserved fruit. There is no reason for concern should this occur, just rinse it off before using.

CHILLI SAMBAL

Use this sambal as a dipping sauce or keep in a jar in the refrigerator to add some quick flavour to your recipes.

Makes 125 mL (4 fl. oz)

- [ ] **25 small red chillies, stalks removed**
- [ ] **2 cloves garlic**
- [ ] **1 small onion, chopped**
- [ ] **2 tablespoons brown sugar**
- [ ] **185 mL (6 fl. oz) water**
- [ ] **1 teaspoon cornflour**
- [ ] **2 tablespoons white vinegar**

1   Place whole chillies, garlic and onion in a food processor or blender and process to make a paste. Transfer to a small saucepan and stir in sugar, water, cornflour and vinegar. Bring to the boil, reduce heat and simmer until thickened.
2   Remove from heat and set aside to cool. Transfer to a warm sterilised jar. Seal and label when cold. Store in the refrigerator until required.

MINT CHUTNEY

The food processor makes the preparation of this chutney very easy. The chutney will keep for up to a week in the refrigerator, and though it loses colour after the first day it still tastes great.

Makes 125 mL (4 fl. oz)

- [ ] **125 g (4 oz) fresh mint sprigs**
- [ ] **3 green chillies, seeds removed and chopped**
- [ ] **3 shallots, chopped**
- [ ] **2 teaspoons sugar**
- [ ] **1/2 teaspoon salt**
- [ ] **1 tablespoon vinegar**

1   Remove mint leaves from stalks. Wash and dry.
2   Place mint leaves, chilli, shallots, sugar, salt and vinegar in a food processor or blender and process until smooth.
3   Transfer to a warm sterilised jar. Seal and store in the refrigerator until required.

DATE AND ORANGE CHUTNEY

A delicious sweet chutney that can also be made using fresh figs rather than dates if you wish.

Makes 500 mL (16 fl. oz)

- [ ] **250 g (8 oz) fresh dates, pitted and chopped**
- [ ] **1 orange, peeled and chopped**
- [ ] **1 teaspoon grated fresh ginger**
- [ ] **60 g (2 oz) raisins**
- [ ] **1 tablespoon brown sugar**
- [ ] **75 mL (21/2 fl. oz) cider vinegar**
- [ ] **75 mL (21/2 fl. oz) water**

1   Place dates, orange, ginger, raisins, sugar, vinegar and water in a saucepan and cook, stirring occasionally, over a low heat for 20 minutes.
2   Transfer to warm sterilised jars, seal and label when cold. Store in the refrigerator until required.

PRESERVING TIPS

❖   There are a few tips you should remember when making pickles, chutneys and other preserves to ensure that your preserves keep well and taste great.
❖   Always use clean unchipped jars.
❖   Remove any old labels by soaking.
❖   The jars must be sterilised before filling or the preserve will go mouldy.
❖   To sterilise jars, wash in hot water then warm in the oven at a low temperature until dry. Remember that the lids must also be sterilised.
❖   Jars should be warm when adding the hot preserve. Cold jars will crack or break if a hot mixture is suddenly added to them.

CHILLI PICKLED CABBAGE

Traditional Kim Chee is made months in advance and is placed in large stone jars to mature. This simplified version is ready after one week.

Makes 1.2L (2 pts)

- ☐ **1 kg (2 lb) Chinese cabbage, coarsely chopped**
- ☐ **1 tablespoon salt**
- ☐ **2 spring onions, chopped**
- ☐ **2 cloves garlic, crushed**
- ☐ **1 tablespoon sambal oelek**
- ☐ **2 teaspoons grated fresh ginger**
- ☐ **125 mL (4 fl.oz) light soy sauce**
- ☐ **125 mL (4 fl.oz) white vinegar**
- ☐ **¹/₂ teaspoon sesame oil**

1   Sprinkle cabbage with salt and set aside for 4 hours.
2   Press cabbage to remove excess liquid. Add spring onions, garlic, sambal oelek, ginger, soy sauce and vinegar, stir to combine.
3   Place into a large, warm, sterilized jar, seal and leave in a cool place for at least 1 day before using to allow flavours to develop.
4   Sprinkle with the sesame oil to serve.

❖

MIDDLE EASTERN PEACH

An exotic pickle that combines the flavours of lush peaches with spices of the Middle East.

Makes 375 mL (12 fl. oz)

- ☐ **1¹/₂ teaspoons tamarind paste**
- ☐ **375 mL (12 fl.oz) white wine vinegar**
- ☐ **500 g (1 lb) fresh peaches, peeled and sliced**
- ☐ **1 tablespoon grated fresh ginger**
- ☐ **3 teaspoons ground coriander**
- ☐ **3 cloves garlic, crushed**
- ☐ **125 g (4 oz) sugar**
- ☐ **2 small red chillies**

1   Dissolve tamarind paste in 125 mL (4 fl. oz) vinegar. Place peaches, ginger, coriander, garlic, tamarind mixture, remaining vinegar, sugar and chillies in a saucepan. Bring to the boil, stirring until sugar is dissolved.
2   Reduce heat and simmer without stirring for 20 minutes. Transfer to warm, sterilised jars. Seal and label when cold.

CURRIED EGGPLANT PICKLE

Blend your own spices to create this perky pickle. Adjust the amount of chilli according to the degree of hotness you desire.

Makes 1.5 L (2¹/₂ pts)

- ☐ **4 small red chillies, seeded and deveined**
- ☐ **5 cloves garlic**
- ☐ **1 tablespoon grated fresh ginger**
- ☐ **1¹/₂ tablespoons mustard seeds**
- ☐ **2 teaspoons ground turmeric**
- ☐ **2 teaspoons garam masala**
- ☐ **250 mL (8 fl. oz) vegetable oil**
- ☐ **1.5 kg (3 lb) eggplant, cut into 2 cm cubes**
- ☐ **¹/₂ teaspoon salt**
- ☐ **125 g (4 oz) brown sugar**
- ☐ **185 mL (6 fl.oz) white vinegar**

1   Blend chillies, garlic, ginger, mustard seeds, turmeric and garam masala to a paste in a food processor or blender.
2   Heat oil in a frypan and cook spice paste for 1 minute. Add eggplant, toss to coat with spice paste. Reduce heat, cover and cook until eggplant is tender. Add salt, sugar and vinegar and simmer, uncovered, until thickened.
3   Transfer to warm sterilised jars. Allow to cool and skim off any oil that rises to the surface. Seal and label when cold.

Left: Mint Chutney, Date and Orange Chutney, Chilli Sambal, Chilli Pickled Cabbage
Below: Middle Eastern Peach, Curried Eggplant Pickle

Delicious Desserts

When special effort has been put into a production, everyone expects a curtain call. Similarly, super meals and parties should be rounded off with splendid desserts, and we've especially chosen ones that complement the varied main course dishes featured in this book.

Figs with Toffee and Warm Rum Sauce, Passionfruit Souffle with Nectarine Cream

FIGS WITH TOFFEE AND WARM RUM SAUCE

Luscious figs served on a creamy sauce are sure to tickle the tastebuds even after the hottest meal.

Serves 4

☐ **4 fresh figs, cut into quarters**

TOFFEE
☐ **375 g (12 oz) sugar**
☐ **375 mL (12 fl. oz) water**

SAUCE
☐ **6 egg yolks**
☐ **185 g (6 oz) caster sugar**
☐ **3 tablespoons rum**
☐ **315 mL (10 fl. oz) cream**

1　To make toffee, place sugar and water in a saucepan, stir over a low heat until sugar dissolves, brushing down crystals from sides of pan with a brush dipped in hot water. Bring to the boil and boil rapidly until toffee turns a golden brown. Remove from heat and stand saucepan in cold water. Allow bubbles to subside and pour toffee onto an oiled baking tray. Set aside to set.

2　To make sauce, just prior to serving, place egg yolks, sugar and rum in the top of a double boiler. Cook over simmering water, beating continuously with an electric beater until sugar dissolves and mixture is creamy. Whisk in cream and continue to cook until sauce is heated through.

3　To serve, break toffee into splinters, spoon sauce into dessert bowls and place figs in the centre. Decorate with toffee.

DON'T BURN IT

When making the toffee for this delicious dessert be very careful not to burn it. You must watch it all the time, as it only takes seconds for the toffee to burn. Once burnt the toffee will have a bitter taste and look unattractive.

PASSIONFRUIT SOUFFLE WITH NECTARINE CREAM

Individual souffles are the perfect dessert after a rich or spicy main meal. While the actual cooking of the souffles has to be left until just before serving, the Nectarine Cream and preparation of the dishes can be prepared in advance.

Serves 4

☐ **softened butter**
☐ **caster sugar**
☐ **125 g (4 fl. oz) passionfruit pulp**
☐ **75 g (2¹/₂ oz) icing sugar, plus 2 tablespoons**
☐ **2 egg yolks**
☐ **1 tablespoon orange juice**
☐ **6 egg whites**

NECTARINE CREAM
☐ **2 very ripe nectarines, skinned and stone removed**
☐ **315mL (10 fl. oz) cream**
☐ **2 tablespoons icing sugar**
☐ **2 tablespoons Grand Marnier**
☐ **icing sugar for dusting**

1　Brush four individual souffle dishes (about 375 mL (12 fl. oz) capacity), with butter and sprinkle with caster sugar. Turn upside down to allow excess sugar to fall out.

2　Place passionfruit pulp, 80 g (2¹/₂ oz) icing sugar, egg yolks and orange juice in a large bowl, mix well to combine.

3　Beat egg whites until soft peaks form, add remaining icing sugar and beat until just combined. Do not overbeat. Fold about a quarter of the egg white mixture into the passionfruit mixture, then gently fold in remaining egg whites. Spoon into souffle dishes. Bake at 180°C (350°F) for 8 minutes or until well-risen.

4　To make Nectarine Cream, puree nectarine flesh in a food processor or blender. Combine cream, icing sugar and Grand Marnier in a bowl and beat until soft peaks form. Gently fold through nectarine puree. Refrigerate until ready to serve.

5　To serve, dust souffles with icing sugar and accompany with a bowl of Nectarine Cream.

STRAWBERRY PRALINE PARFAIT

A spectacular dessert that can be prepared in advance. Sprinkle the final quantity of praline just before serving to ensure a crunchy topping.

Serves 4

- ☐ **500 g (1 lb) strawberries**
- ☐ **2 tablespoons Grand Marnier**
- ☐ **2 tablespoons caster sugar**

CUSTARD
- ☐ **250 mL (8 fl. oz) milk**
- ☐ **125 mL (4 fl. oz) cream**
- ☐ **vanilla bean**
- ☐ **4 egg yolks**
- ☐ **2 tablespoons cornflour**
- ☐ **75 g (2 ^{1}/$_2$ oz) caster sugar**

PRALINE CREAM
- ☐ **185 g (6 oz) sugar**
- ☐ **90 g (3 oz) roasted hazelnuts**

GRAND MARNIER CREAM
- ☐ **250 mL (8 fl. oz) cream**
- ☐ **2 tablespoons icing sugar**
- ☐ **2 tablespoons Grand Marnier**

1   To make custard, place milk, cream and vanilla bean in a saucepan. Cook over medium heat until mixture comes to the boil. Remove from heat and set aside for 5 minutes.

2   Place egg yolks, cornflour and sugar in a bowl and beat until combined. Remove vanilla bean from milk mixture and gradually pour onto egg yolk mixture, beating until combined. Cook, stirring over low heat, until sauce thickens. Remove from heat and set aside to cool. Place plastic food wrap or greaseproof paper over custard to prevent skin from forming. Refrigerate until ready to serve.

3   To make praline, place sugar in shallow frypan, stand over medium heat and allow to melt, stirring occasionally until completely melted and golden brown. Spread hazelnuts in a lightly oiled shallow cake pan, pour over toffee and set aside to cool. Break up toffee and place in a food processor fitted with a metal blade. Process to break toffee and nuts into small pieces.

4   Place strawberries, Grand Marnier and icing sugar in a bowl. Toss to combine and refrigerate for 30 minutes.

5   To make cream, place cream, icing sugar and Grand Marnier in a bowl and beat until soft peaks form. Fold half the praline through the cream. Refrigerate until ready to serve.

6   To assemble dessert, spoon equal quantities of custard into base of four serving glasses. Top with a third of the praline, arrange drained strawberries on top. Sprinkle with half the remaining praline. Spoon over Grand Marnier cream and top with remaining praline.

❖

PEACH FRITTERS WITH COCONUT SAUCE

Fragrant and delicious, these peach fritters are a treat. For a delightful change, use halved apricots instead of quartered peaches and prepare in the same way.

Serves 4

- ☐ **155 g (5 oz) flour, sifted**
- ☐ **pinch salt**
- ☐ **1 egg, lightly beaten**
- ☐ **2 tablespoons beer**
- ☐ **4 peaches, peeled, quartered and stones removed**
- ☐ **60 mL (2 fl. oz) Amaretto liqueur**
- ☐ **2 egg whites**
- ☐ **hot oil for deep frying**
- ☐ **caster sugar**

SAUCE
- ☐ **125 mL (4 fl. oz) coconut cream**
- ☐ **60 g (2 oz) sugar**
- ☐ **2 tablespoons Amaretto liqueur**
- ☐ **60 mL (2 fl. oz) cream**
- ☐ **toasted shredded coconut, for decoration**

1   Place flour and salt in a bowl, add egg and beer and mix well. Set aside to stand for 2 hours.

2   Place peach quarters in a bowl with liqueur and marinate for 20 minutes. Beat egg whites until stiff peaks form, gently fold through batter.

3   Heat oil in a deep saucepan. Drain peaches and dip a few quarters at a time in the batter. Drop into oil and cook until golden brown, remove and roll in sugar. Repeat with remaining peaches and batter.

4   To make sauce, place coconut cream in a saucepan and cook over a low heat to melt. Add sugar and stir until sugar dissolves. Add liqueur and cream and cook over a medium heat stirring until sauce boils. Reduce heat and simmer for 1 minute. Remove from heat and set aside to cool slightly.

5   To serve, spoon sauce onto individual serving plates, top with fritters and sprinkle with coconut.

❖

HONEY AND APRICOT ICE CREAM

The perfect dinner party dessert, refreshing and easy to make. Homemade ice cream is best if used within a couple of days of making. Remove ice cream from the freezer and place in the fridge for about 30 minutes before serving. This allows the flavour to develop and makes it easier to serve.

Serves 6

- ☐ **250 g (8 oz) dried apricots**
- ☐ **1 cinnamon stick, crumbled**
- ☐ **3 cloves**
- ☐ **^{1}/$_2$ teaspoon grated nutmeg**
- ☐ **125 g (4 oz) brown sugar**
- ☐ **60 mL (2 oz) honey**
- ☐ **315 mL (10 fl. oz) cups water**
- ☐ **800 mL (1^1/$_4$ pts) unflavoured yoghurt**
- ☐ **250 mL (8 fl. oz) sour cream**

1   Combine apricots, crumbled cinnamon stick, cloves, nutmeg, sugar, honey and water in a saucepan. Cook over a low heat until sugar dissolves. Bring to the boil, reduce heat and simmer, uncovered, for 10 minutes or until apricots soften. Drain apricots, strain liquid, and reserve.

2   Place apricots and reserved liquid in a food processor or blender and puree. Stir in yoghurt and sour cream. Spoon into a freezerproof container and freeze.

Strawberry Praline Parfait, Peach Fritters with Coconut Sauce, Honey and Apricot Ice Cream

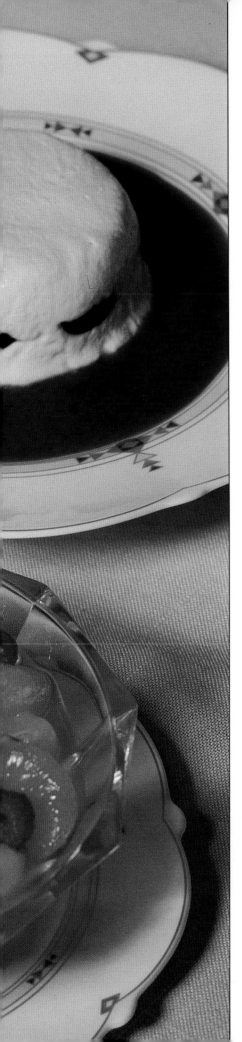

RUM CHERRY CREAM

Serves 6

- ☐ **210 g (6¹/₂ oz) cherries, washed, stoned and halved**
- ☐ **3 tablespoons dark rum**
- ☐ **125 g (4 oz) sugar**
- ☐ **155 g (5 oz) ricotta cheese**
- ☐ **375 g (12 oz) cream cheese**
- ☐ **75mL (2¹/₂ fl. oz) sour cream**

SAUCE
- ☐ **4 large dark plums, skinned, stones removed and halved**
- ☐ **210 g (6¹/₂ oz) loganberries**
- ☐ **2 tablespoons icing sugar**
- ☐ **mint leaves to garnish**

1 Place cherries, 2 tablespoons rum and 1 tablespoon sugar in a bowl and set aside to stand for 1 hour. Pour off rum and dry cherries on absorbent kitchen paper.
2 Press ricotta cheese through a sieve and set aside. Place cream cheese in a bowl and beat until soft and creamy. Beat in remaining sugar, ricotta, sour cream and remaining rum. Continue to beat until well combined.
3 Line six ramekins with damp muslin and half fill with cream mixture. Arrange cherries over the mixture and top with remaining cream. Refrigerate overnight.
4 To make sauce, place plums, berries and icing sugar in a food processor or blender and puree. Push puree through a sieve and refrigerate. To serve, spoon sauce onto serving plate. Turn out creams, remove muslin and place in the centre of the plate. Garnish with mint leaves.

SNOW EGGS WITH PASSIONFRUIT SAUCE

Serves 4

MOUSSE
- ☐ **60 mL (2 fl. oz) champagne**
- ☐ **2¹/₂ teaspoons gelatine**
- ☐ **250 mL (8 fl. oz) boiling water**
- ☐ **60 g (2 oz) caster sugar**
- ☐ **1 tablespoon orange juice**
- ☐ **2 tablespoons Grand Marnier**
- ☐ **1 teaspoon grated orange rind**
- ☐ **3 large egg whites**
- ☐ **pinch cream of tartar**

SAUCE
- ☐ **75 mL (2¹/₂ fl. oz) Sauterne**
- ☐ **185 mL (6 fl. oz) cream**
- ☐ **3 egg yolks**
- ☐ **60 g (2 oz) icing sugar**
- ☐ **125 mL (4 fl. oz) passionfruit pulp**

1 To make mousse, place champagne in a large bowl and sprinkle over gelatine. Set aside to soften for 10 minutes. Add boiling water and half the sugar, stirring until sugar dissolves. Mix in orange juice, Grand Marnier and orange rind. Chill for about 1 hour or until mixture begins to set. Beat until light and frothy.
2 Beat egg whites until frothy, add cream of tartar and continue to beat until soft peaks form. Gradually add remaining sugar and beat until stiff and glossy. Fold through gelatine mixture. Chill until set.
3 To make sauce, combine Sauterne, cream, egg yolks and icing sugar in a saucepan. Cook over a medium heat, whisking until sauce thickens. Stir in passionfruit pulp and mix to combine. Chill well before serving.
4 To serve, using an oval ice cream scoop dipped in hot water, form mousse into an egg shape. Place eggs on four dessert plates and spoon over sauce.

LIQUEUR FRUIT SALAD

Serves 4

- ☐ **¹/₂ pineapple, skinned, cored and cubed**
- ☐ **8 lychees, peeled, halved and seeds removed**
- ☐ **250 g (8 oz) raspberries**
- ☐ **4 mandarins, segmented**
- ☐ **125 mL (4 fl. oz) champagne**

ORANGE SYRUP
- ☐ **1 tablespoon grated orange rind**
- ☐ **1 tablespoon grated lemon rind**
- ☐ **125 g (4 oz) caster sugar**
- ☐ **250 mL (8 fl. oz) water**
- ☐ **125 mL (4 fl. oz) fresh orange juice**
- ☐ **60 mL (2 fl. oz) Grand Marnier**
- ☐ **60 mL (2 fl. oz) passionfruit pulp**

1 To make syrup, place orange rind, lemon rind, sugar and water in saucepan and cook over a low heat until sugar dissolves. Bring to the boil and boil rapidly for 5 minutes. Remove from heat and set aside until cold. Strain and discard rinds. Stir in orange juice, Grand Marnier and passionfruit pulp, mix to combine.
2 Place pineapple, lychees, raspberries and mandarin segments in a bowl. Pour over syrup, cover and set aside to marinate overnight. To serve, drain fruit and place in serving bowl. Pour over champagne.

Snow Eggs with Passionfruit Sauce, Rum Cherry Cream, Liqueur Fruit Salad

Hearty Dishes

*Galoshes and jumpers,
eiderdowns and dressing
gowns, fireplaces and long,
dark afternoons – what's for
dinner! This chapter
concentrates on the types of
flavoursome, robust meals
that memories of home are
made of, so be sure you
make enough to go around
– twice!*

*Creamy Chicken with Sweet Potato,
Bouillabaisse*

BOUILLABAISSE

A tasty medley of all fishy favourites. Serve this one-pot meal with crusty garlic or herbed bread for an informal lunch.

Serves 8

- ☐ **500 g (1 lb) firm boneless fish fillets, cubed**
- ☐ **3 tablespoons olive oil**
- ☐ **4 cloves garlic, crushed**
- ☐ **3 tablespoons lemon juice**
- ☐ **4 tablespoons olive oil, extra**
- ☐ **2 onions, peeled and chopped**
- ☐ **2 large leeks, chopped**
- ☐ **410 g (13 oz) canned tomatoes, crushed**
- ☐ **bouquet garni**
- ☐ **pinch saffron threads**
- ☐ **¹/₂ teaspoon ground black pepper**
- ☐ **600 mL (1 pt) rich fish stock**
- ☐ **2 large uncooked crabs, chopped into pieces (shell on)**
- ☐ **1 green lobster tail, chopped into pieces (shell on)**
- ☐ **16 mussels, uncooked**
- ☐ **3 tablespoons finely chopped parsley**

1   Combine fish, 3 tablespoons oil, garlic and juice in medium bowl. Cover and set aside for 20 minutes.

2   Heat remaining oil in large saucepan. Stir in onions and leeks and cook over low heat for 10 minutes or until soft. Stir in tomatoes, bouquet garni, saffron and pepper. Bring to boil, reduce heat and simmer, covered, for 10 minutes.

3   Stir stock into vegetable sauce. Bring to the boil, reduce heat and simmer, uncovered, for 10 minutes. Add fish and marinade to pan. Stir in crab and lobster, bring to the boil, reduce heat and simmer, uncovered, for 8 minutes. Add mussels to pan and cook until mussels open. Stir in parsley and serve immediately.

DID YOU KNOW?

Bouillabaisse was originally cooked on the beach by fishermen, who used a large cauldron set over a wood fire. The fish used were those less suitable for the market. Traditionally the soup and the fish are served separately, with the soup being poured over slices of dried home-made bread.

CREAMY CHICKEN WITH SWEET POTATO

The combination of chicken and sweet potato with a hint of curry makes a delicious family meal.

Serves 4

- ☐ **3 tablespoons oil**
- ☐ **8 chicken thighs**
- ☐ **3 tablespoons plain flour**
- ☐ **2 onions, sliced**
- ☐ **1 tablespoon mild curry powder**
- ☐ **1 teaspoon brown mustard seeds**
- ☐ **250 mL (8 fl. oz) dry white wine**
- ☐ **250 mL (8 fl. oz) chicken stock**
- ☐ **440 g (14 oz) canned tomatoes, chopped**
- ☐ **500 g (1 lb) sweet potato, peeled and cut into 3 cm (1¹/₂ in) cubes**
- ☐ **2 cloves garlic, crushed**
- ☐ **3 tablespoons finely chopped fresh basil**
- ☐ **2 tablespoons mayonnaise**
- ☐ **2 tablespoons sour cream**

1   Heat oil in large saucepan. Toss chicken pieces in flour. Add to pan and cook over medium heat until browned. Remove from pan and drain on absorbent paper. Set aside and keep warm.

2   Add onions to pan, cook over low heat for 5 minutes or until soft. Stir in curry powder and mustard seeds, cook for 2 minutes stirring continually. Stir in wine, chicken stock and tomatoes, bring to boil then reduce heat.

3   Return chicken to saucepan and add sweet potato. Simmer, covered, for about 30 minutes or until chicken is cooked and potato is tender. Combine garlic, basil, mayonnaise and sour cream in small bowl. Add to saucepan, stirring over low heat until just warmed through. Season to taste.

PORK HOCK RISOTTO

Earthy and comforting, this substantial risotto makes an ideal midwinter meal.

Serves 8

- ☐ 3 tablespoons butter
- ☐ 4 medium pork hocks
- ☐ 1 L (1³/₄ pts) water
- ☐ 1 bouquet garni
- ☐ 1 teaspoon whole black peppercorns
- ☐ 2 eggplants, unpeeled, chopped
- ☐ salt
- ☐ 375 g (12 oz) long grain rice
- ☐ 375 mL (12 fl. oz) chicken stock
- ☐ 1 onion, chopped
- ☐ 1 teaspoon ground turmeric
- ☐ 2 green capsicums, sliced
- ☐ 2 tomatoes, peeled, seeded and chopped
- ☐ chopped fresh herbs, such as parsley, chives and coriander

1   Heat butter in large saucepan. Add hocks and cook over high heat until browned all over. Stir in water, bouquet garni and peppercorns. Bring to the boil, reduce heat and simmer, covered, for 1 hour.

2   Sprinkle eggplant liberally with salt, set aside for 20 minutes. Rinse under cold running water and pat dry with absorbent kitchen paper.

3   Remove meat from the hocks and transfer with liquid to a deep casserole dish. Stir in rice, stock, onion and turmeric, cover and cook at 180°C (350°F) for 50 minutes. Remove bouquet garni and discard.

4   Add eggplant, capsicums and tomato to casserole and cook, uncovered, for 10 minutes or until almost all liquid is absorbed and rice is tender. Stand for 5 minutes and sprinkle with fresh herbs before serving.

TASTY VEAL AND POTATO BAKE

Serves 6

- ☐ 3 tablespoons butter
- ☐ 12 veal loin chops, boned and rolled
- ☐ 1 onion, finely chopped
- ☐ 3 whole cloves
- ☐ 1 cardamom pod, bruised
- ☐ ¹/₂ teaspoon cumin seeds
- ☐ ¹/₂ teaspoon coriander seeds
- ☐ 1 teaspoon black peppercorns
- ☐ 2 cloves garlic, chopped
- ☐ 410 g (13 oz) canned tomato puree
- ☐ 500 mL (16 fl. oz) beef stock
- ☐ 2 tablespoons tomato sauce
- ☐ 2 potatoes, peeled and parboiled
- ☐ 2 tablespoons butter, melted

1   Heat butter in large frypan. Add meat and cook until browned on all sides. Remove from pan and arrange in a shallow ovenproof dish, cover and keep warm.

2   Add onion, cloves, cardamom, cumin,

coriander, peppercorns and garlic to pan and cook over low heat for 5 minutes or until onion is soft. Stir in tomato puree, stock and sauce, bring to the boil and simmer, uncovered, for about 20 minutes or until sauce has thickened slightly, stirring occasionally. Strain sauce through fine sieve and pour over veal.

3   Slice potatoes thinly, arrange over veal. Drizzle with butter and bake, uncovered, at 200°C (400°F) for 25–30 minutes or until veal is tender and potatoes are golden.

WHICH TARRAGON?

There are two types of tarragon – French and Russian. While they look very similar, the Russian tarragon has a coarser leaf and is virtually tasteless.
✧ Tarragon is a herb which is best used fresh, as its essential oils are volatile and are lost in drying. When a recipe calls for tarragon it usually refers to French tarragon.

❖

TARRAGON PORK WITH VEGETABLES

A succulent pot roast of pork with vegetables delicately flavoured with fresh tarragon.

Serves 6

- ☐ **2 tablespoons butter**
- ☐ **1 kg (2 lb) boned and rolled shoulder of pork**
- ☐ **2 onions, chopped**
- ☐ **1 leek, chopped**
- ☐ **750 mL (1¼ pt) chicken stock**
- ☐ **3 tablespoons lemon juice**
- ☐ **1 teaspoon cracked black pepper**
- ☐ **2 dried bay leaves**
- ☐ **1 turnip, peeled and chopped**
- ☐ **12 baby potatoes, washed and drained**
- ☐ **2 carrots, peeled and chopped**
- ☐ **2 sticks celery, chopped**
- ☐ **3 tablespoons redcurrant jelly**
- ☐ **2 tablespoons chopped fresh tarragon**

1   Heat butter in large saucepan. Add pork and cook over high heat until browned on all sides. Add onions and leek to pan with meat and cook over low heat for 5 minutes or until onion softens.

2   Add stock, lemon juice, pepper and bay leaves, bring to the boil. Reduce heat and simmer, covered, for 30 minutes turning meat occasionally. Add turnip, potatoes, carrots and celery and simmer, covered, for 15 minutes longer or until vegetables are firm but tender and meat is cooked through.

3   Remove meat and vegetables from pan. Set aside and keep warm. Bring pan juices to the boil and boil, uncovered, for 2 minutes. Stir in redcurrant jelly and tarragon and simmer for 5 minutes. To serve, slice pork, accompany with vegetables and spoon over sauce.

Left: Pork Hock Risotto
Above: Tasty Veal and Potato Bake, Tarragon Pork with Vegetables

TOMATO AND THYME SHANKS

Served either hot or cold, these lamb shanks are a delicious and filling family meal. When cooked, the meat should be very tender and almost falling off the bone.

Serves 4

- ☐ **4 lamb shanks**
- ☐ **2 shallots, chopped**
- ☐ **1 red capsicum, chopped**
- ☐ **250 mL (8 fl. oz) tomato sauce**
- ☐ **125 mL (4 fl. oz) cider vinegar**
- ☐ **250 mL (8 fl. oz) water**
- ☐ **1 clove garlic, crushed**
- ☐ **1 teaspoon finely chopped fresh thyme**
- ☐ **freshly ground black pepper**

1   Place shanks, shallots and capsicum in a large casserole dish. Combine tomato sauce, vinegar, water, garlic and thyme and pour over shanks.
2   Cover and bake at 150 °C (300°F) for 2^1/2 hours or until meat is very tender. Season to taste with pepper. Serve immediately or allow to cool and serve at room temperature.

PAPRIKA BEEF

Chunks of beef are marinated and then cooked in a flavoursome liquid. Remember, the longer your meat is in the marinade, the more tasty and tender it will be.

Serves 8

- ☐ **1 kg (2 lb) chuck steak, cut into 2.5 cm (1 in) squares**
- ☐ **4 tablespoons oil**
- ☐ **2 onions, peeled, sliced**
- ☐ **125 mL (4 fl. oz) dry white wine**
- ☐ **250 mL (8 fl. oz) water**
- ☐ **185 g (6 oz) stuffed Spanish olives**
- ☐ **4 tablespoons chopped fresh flat leafed parsley**

MARINADE
- ☐ **1 teaspoon ground turmeric**
- ☐ **1^1/2 tablespoons mild paprika**
- ☐ **^{1}/2 teaspoon chilli powder**
- ☐ **220 g (7 oz) plain natural yoghurt**
- ☐ **2 teaspoons grated lemon rind**

Tomato and Thyme Shanks, Paprika Beef, Lamb Pot Roast

1   To make marinade, combine turmeric, paprika, chilli powder, yoghurt and rind in bowl. Add steak and toss to coat. Cover and refrigerate for 2–4 hours or overnight.
2   Heat oil in large saucepan. Add onions and cook over medium heat for about 5 minutes or until onions soften. Add steak and marinade and cook over high heat for about 10 minutes or until steak is well browned.
3   Stir in wine and water. Bring to the boil, cover and simmer for about 1^1/2 hours or until steak is tender. Stir in olives and parsley, cook over medium heat for 3 minutes longer. Season to taste.

LAMB POT ROAST

An adaptation of a Middle Eastern recipe that traditionally would have been prepared at home and then taken to the local baker's oven for cooking.

Serves 6

- ☐ **2 kg (4 lb) leg lamb**
- ☐ **2 cloves garlic, crushed**
- ☐ **6 small sprigs fresh rosemary**
- ☐ **freshly ground black pepper**
- ☐ **6 potatoes, peeled and halved lengthways**
- ☐ **2 tablespoons lemon juice**
- ☐ **4 tomatoes, peeled and chopped**
- ☐ **2 onions, chopped**
- ☐ **125 mL (4 fl. oz) chicken stock**
- ☐ **3 tablespoons dry vermouth**
- ☐ **1 cm (^{1}/2 in) piece lemon peel**
- ☐ **small piece cinnamon stick**
- ☐ **2 tablespoons butter**

1   Cut slits in the surface of the lamb with a sharp knife. Insert garlic slivers and rosemary sprigs. Dust with pepper and place in a roasting pan. Bake at 180°C (350°F) for 1 hour. Remove pan from oven and drain off pan juices.
2   Cut potato halves part way down through rounded side. Brush with lemon juice and arrange around lamb. Top with tomatoes and onions. Combine stock and vermouth and pour over lamb and vegetables. Add the lemon peel and cinnamon stick. Dot with butter and bake at 180°C (350°F) for 1^1/2 hours longer.
3   Remove lamb from roasting pan. Wrap in aluminium foil and stand for 15 minutes before carving. Skim any excess fat from pan contents. To serve, slice meat and accompany with potatoes and tomato and onion sauce.

HEARTY VEGETABLE SOUP

Serves 8

- ☐ **2 tablespoons butter**
- ☐ **250 g (8 oz) button mushrooms**
- ☐ **2 medium carrots, sliced**
- ☐ **1 large leek, chopped**
- ☐ **1.5 L (2¹/₂ pts) rich chicken stock**
- ☐ **250 g (8 oz) pasta elbows**
- ☐ **1 red capsicum, chopped**
- ☐ **2 tablespoons dark soy sauce**
- ☐ **3 leaves English spinach, finely shredded**
- ☐ **¹/₂ cup finely chopped parsley**
- ☐ **¹/₂ teaspoon Mexican chilli powder**
- ☐ **freshly grated Parmesan cheese**

1 Heat butter in large saucepan. Add mushrooms and carrots. Cook over low heat for 5 minutes, stirring constantly.

2 Add leek and stock, bring to the boil. Stir in pasta, simmer, uncovered, for 12 minutes or until pasta is almost cooked.

3 Add capsicum and soy sauce, simmer for 5 minutes longer. Stir in spinach, parsley and chilli powder just before serving. Serve soup with freshly grated Parmesan cheese.

BABY OCTOPUS IN RED WINE

Serves 6

- ☐ **1 kg (2 lb) baby octopus**
- ☐ **3 tablespoons polyunsaturated oil**
- ☐ **6 shallots, chopped**
- ☐ **2 cloves garlic, crushed**
- ☐ **125 mL (4 fl. oz) dry red wine**
- ☐ **125 mL (4 fl. oz) chicken stock**
- ☐ **440 g (14 oz) canned tomatoes, undrained and mashed**
- ☐ **1 teaspoon grated lemon rind**
- ☐ **freshly ground black pepper**
- ☐ **2 tablespoons finely chopped coriander**

1 Remove tentacles, intestines and ink sac from octopus. Cut out the eyes and beak. Remove skin and rinse well.

2 Place octopus in a large saucepan, cover and simmer for 15 minutes. Drain off any juices and set aside to cool slightly.

3 Heat oil in a saucepan and cook shallots for 2–3 minutes. Add garlic and octopus and cook for 4–5 minutes. Pour wine into pan and cook over medium heat, until almost all the wine has evaporated.

4 Combine stock, tomatoes, lemon rind, pepper and coriander. Cover and simmer gently for 1¹/₂ hours until octopus is tender.

BEEF WITH PUMPKIN AND LEMON GRASS

Serve this unusual and flavoursome dish accompanied by bowls of unflavoured yoghurt and topped with freshly chopped coriander.

Serves 4

- ☐ **2 tablespoons oil**
- ☐ **2 onions, chopped**
- ☐ **1 teaspoon whole allspice**
- ☐ **1 cinnamon stick**
- ☐ **1 teaspoon grated fresh ginger**
- ☐ **2 green capsicums, sliced**
- ☐ **750 g (1¹/₂ lb) chuck steak, cut into 4 cm cubes**
- ☐ **2 tablespoons chopped fresh lemon grass**
- ☐ **500 mL (16 fl. oz) chicken stock**
- ☐ **500 g (1 lb) pumpkin, peeled, cut into 4 cm (1¹/₂ in) cubes**
- ☐ **2 cloves garlic, crushed**

1   Heat oil in large heavy based saucepan. Cook onions over medium heat until golden. Stir in allspice, cinnamon, ginger and capsicum.

2   Add meat to pan, cook over high heat until browned. Stir in lemon grass and chicken stock. Bring to the boil, reduce heat and simmer, covered, for 45 minutes.

3   Stir in pumpkin, cover and simmer for 45 minutes or until beef is tender. Remove from heat and stir in garlic. Season to taste.

❖

SEASONED SAUSAGE RAGOUT

For a complete meal, serve this tasty ragout with a chilled tomato salad and crusty French bread.

Serves 6

- ☐ **500 g (1lb) veal mince**
- ☐ **60 g (2 oz) finely chopped fresh parsley**
- ☐ **60 g (2 oz) finely chopped fresh basil**
- ☐ **3 tablespoons pine nuts**
- ☐ **1 tablespoon olive oil**
- ☐ **2 cloves garlic, crushed**
- ☐ **1 teaspoon cracked black pepper**
- ☐ **185 g (6 oz) fresh breadcrumbs**
- ☐ **60 g (2 oz) grated fresh Parmesan cheese**
- ☐ **seasoned flour**
- ☐ **oil for deep frying**
- ☐ **3 tablespoons soy sauce**
- ☐ **125 mL (4 fl. oz) lemon juice**
- ☐ **250 mL (8 fl. oz) chicken stock**
- ☐ **250 mL (8 fl. oz) dry white wine**
- ☐ **12 whole baby potatoes, scrubbed**
- ☐ **12 whole baby onions, peeled**
- ☐ **3 tablespoons chopped fresh basil**

1   Combine mince, parsley, basil, nuts, oil, garlic, pepper, breadcrumbs and cheese in large bowl, mix until well combined. Shape into 12 sausages, 10cm (4in) long. Roll in seasoned flour.

2   Heat oil in deep frypan. Cook sausages a few at a time until browned but not cooked through. Remove sausages and drain on absorbent kitchen paper. Repeat with remaining sausages.

3   Arrange sausages, potatoes and onions in deep saucepan. Combine soy sauce, juice, stock, wine and basil in bowl, pour into saucepan. Bring to the boil, reduce heat and simmer, covered, for 20 minutes or until potatoes are tender. Thicken sauce in pan, if desired.

Above: Beef with Pumpkin and Lemon Grass, Seasoned Sausage Ragout
Left: Hearty Vegetable Soup, Baby Octopus in Red Wine

BAKED EGGPLANT WITH LAMB

Serves 8

- ☐ 8 long eggplants, each about 125g (4oz)
- ☐ salt
- ☐ 500 g (1 lb) lean minced lamb
- ☐ 1 onion, finely chopped
- ☐ 1 clove garlic, crushed
- ☐ freshly ground black pepper
- ☐ 1 small red capsicum, seeded and chopped
- ☐ 2 tablespoons finely chopped fresh basil
- ☐ $^1/_2$ teaspoon dried oregano
- ☐ $^1/_4$ teaspoon chilli powder
- ☐ 125 mL (4 fl. oz) tomato puree
- ☐ 125 mL (4 fl. oz) chicken stock
- ☐ 4 tablespoons grated Parmesan cheese
- ☐ 2 tablespoons butter

1   Remove stems from eggplants. Cut almost through eggplants crosswise at 2 cm ($^3/_4$ in) intervals, taking care not to cut right through. Sprinkle salt liberally onto cut surfaces and set aside for 30 minutes. Rinse in cold water and pat dry on absorbent paper.
2   Combine lamb, onion, garlic, pepper, capsicum, basil, oregano and chilli powder. Stuff some meat mixture in each cut of the eggplants, filling generously. Place filled eggplants in a baking pan.
3   Blend tomato puree and stock together and pour over eggplants. Top with cheese and dot with butter. Bake at 180°C (350°F) for 45 minutes, basting with pan juices during cooking.

BEAN STEW

Serves 6

- ☐ 2 tablespoons olive oil
- ☐ 1 large onion, thinly sliced
- ☐ 3 bacon rashers, chopped
- ☐ 1 carrot, peeled and chopped
- ☐ 1 stick celery, chopped
- ☐ 1 red capsicum, chopped
- ☐ 1 dried bay leaf
- ☐ 1 teaspoon ground cinnamon
- ☐ 250 mL (8 fl. oz) tomato puree
- ☐ 250 mL (8 fl. oz) water
- ☐ 410 g (13 oz) canned butter beans, rinsed and drained
- ☐ 410 g (13 oz) canned red kidney beans, rinsed and drained
- ☐ 2 tablespoons chopped fresh coriander

1   Heat oil in medium saucepan. Add onion and bacon, cook over low heat for 5 minutes or until onion softens. Add carrot, celery, capsicum, bay leaf, cinnamon, puree and water. Bring to the boil and simmer, covered, for 5 minutes.
2   Stir in beans and coriander, bring to the boil and simmer, uncovered, for 10 minutes. Season to taste.

FRUITY CHICKEN CASSEROLE

This Middle Eastern inspired casserole looks great served on a bed of saffron rice and garnished with fresh thyme sprigs.

Serves 6

- ☐ 12 chicken wings, rinsed and drained
- ☐ 3 tablespoons oil
- ☐ 3 tablespoons plain flour
- ☐ 2 onions, sliced
- ☐ 12 baby potatoes, scrubbed
- ☐ 250 mL (8 fl. oz) chicken stock
- ☐ 250 mL (8 fl. oz) apple juice or cider
- ☐ 125 mL (4 fl. oz) lemon juice
- ☐ 125 mL (4 fl. oz) honey
- ☐ 220 g (7 oz) whole dried apricots
- ☐ 220 g (7 oz) dried apples, chopped
- ☐ 90 g (3 oz) prunes, pitted
- ☐ 12 black olives
- ☐ 1 tablespoon chopped fresh lemon thyme

1   Lightly coat chicken with flour. Heat oil in large saucepan, add chicken pieces and cook over medium heat for 8 minutes or until golden brown. Remove from pan and drain on absorbent kitchen paper.
2   Add onions and potatoes to pan, cook over low heat for about 5 minutes or until onion softens. Stir in stock, juices and honey. Return chicken to pan, add apricots, apples and prunes. Bring mixture to the boil and simmer, covered, for 20 minutes or until chicken and fruits are tender.
3   Just before serving, stir in olives and thyme. Season to taste.

Baked Eggplant with Lamb, Bean Stew, Fruity Chicken Casserole

Mild Dishes

These dishes may be mild, but they're certainly not meek. We've taken a new and bold look at vegetables and turned them into dumplings. We've put chicken in our omelette, and cous cous in our veal casserole and large smiles on everybody's faces.

Vegetable Dumplings with Yoghurt Sauce, Mixed Satays

VEGETABLE DUMPLINGS WITH YOGHURT SAUCE

Hearty vegetable dumplings served with a mildly spiced sauce make an interesting vegetarian meal.

Serves 6

- ☐ 1 cup dried chick peas
- ☐ 2 large old potatoes, peeled, chopped
- ☐ 1 carrot, grated finely
- ☐ 1 tablespoon mild curry paste
- ☐ 1 tablespoon unflavoured yoghurt
- ☐ 90 g (3 oz) plain flour
- ☐ 2 tablespoons finely chopped fresh coriander
- ☐ 500 mL (16 fl. oz) light chicken stock

YOGHURT SAUCE
- ☐ 220 g (7 oz) unflavoured yoghurt
- ☐ 1 tablespoon sugar
- ☐ 1 teaspoon mixed spice
- ☐ $^1/_2$ teaspoon ground chilli powder
- ☐ $^1/_2$ teaspoon ground cumin
- ☐ 2 tablespoons finely chopped fresh coriander
- ☐ 1 teaspoon curry paste

1 Place chick peas in a large bowl and cover with boiling water. Set aside to stand overnight. Rinse and drain chick peas. Place into medium saucepan and cover with water. Bring to the boil, simmer, covered for 20 minutes or until peas are almost tender. Add potatoes and cook until soft. Remove from heat, drain and mash with a fork.

2 Combine pea mixture, carrot, paste, 45 g (1$^1/_2$ oz) flour, yoghurt and coriander. Using wet hands, mould into oval shapes 5 cm long. Roll in remaining flour. Refrigerate for 20 minutes.

3 Bring stock to the boil in medium saucepan. Cook dumplings a few at a time in stock, for 5 minutes or until dumplings float to the surface. Using a slotted spoon, remove dumplings from stock, set aside and keep warm while cooking remaining dumplings.

4 To make sauce, combine yoghurt, sugar, mixed spice, chilli powder, cumin, coriander and curry paste in a medium bowl. Cover and set aside for 20 minutes. Serve with dumplings.

MIXED SATAYS

Throw an Oriental influenced barbecue and make these satay skewers the stars of the party.

Serves 4

- ☐ 220 g (7 oz) rump steak, cut into thin strips
- ☐ 220 g (7 oz) pork fillets, cut into thin strips
- ☐ 220 g (7 oz) chicken thigh fillets, skinned, cut into thin strips
- ☐ $^1/_2$ teaspoon chilli powder
- ☐ 2 tablespoons hoisin sauce
- ☐ $^1/_2$ teaspoon ground coriander
- ☐ $^1/_2$ teaspoon ground cumin
- ☐ 1 teaspoon ground turmeric
- ☐ 1 teaspoon garam masala
- ☐ 1 tablespoon sugar
- ☐ 1 tablespoon lime juice
- ☐ shredded lettuce

SATAY SAUCE
- ☐ $^1/_2$ cup crunchy peanut butter
- ☐ 1 onion, peeled, chopped
- ☐ 2 tablespoons hoisin sauce
- ☐ 2 cloves garlic, crushed
- ☐ 185 mL (6 fl. oz) coconut milk
- ☐ 2 tablespoons finely chopped fresh coriander

1 Combine steak, pork, chicken, chilli powder, hoisin, coriander, cumin, turmeric, garam masala, sugar and lime juice in a bowl. Cover and refrigerate for 2–4 hours or overnight.

2 Thread meats alternately onto bamboo skewers. Grill or barbecue over high heat for 5 minutes or until meats are cooked to taste. Turn twice during cooking.

3 To make sauce, place peanut butter, onion, hoisin, garlic and milk in food processor or blender and process until smooth. Stir in coriander. To serve, place skewers on a bed of shredded lettuce and top with satay sauce.

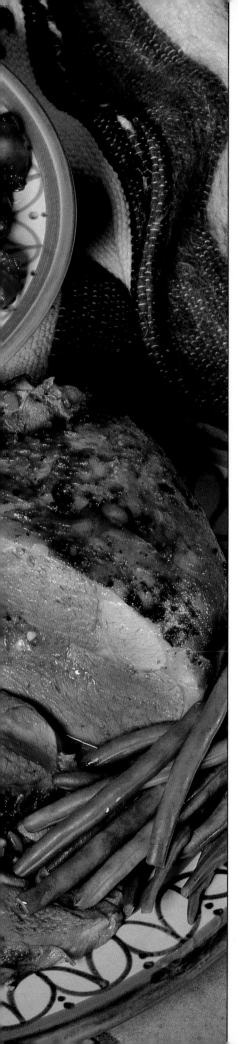

VEAL COUS COUS CASSEROLE

A tasty casserole reminiscent of Morocco is just as good made with lamb.

Serves 6

- ☐ **125 g (4 oz) cous cous**
- ☐ **2 tablespoons oil**
- ☐ **2 onions, peeled, sliced**
- ☐ **$^1/_2$ teaspoon cardamom seeds**
- ☐ **2 teaspoons brown mustard seeds**
- ☐ **2 cinnamon sticks**
- ☐ **4 dried curry leaves**
- ☐ **500 g (1lb) minced veal**
- ☐ **1 tablespoon tomato paste**
- ☐ **410 g (13 oz) canned tomatoes, crushed**
- ☐ **250 mL (8 fl. oz) chicken stock**
- ☐ **1 green capsicum, chopped**
- ☐ **125 g (4 oz) canned corn kernels, drained**

1 Place cous cous in heatproof bowl and cover with boiling water. Set aside for 1 hour or until all liquid is absorbed.
2 Heat oil in medium saucepan. Add onions, seeds, cinnamon stick and curry leaves, cook stirring until onions soften and seeds begin to pop. Add mince and cook over high heat, until veal is well browned. Mix in tomato paste, tomatoes and stock. Bring to the boil and simmer, uncovered for 5 minutes.
3 Add capsicum, corn and cous cous to saucepan, mix well to combine. Cover and simmer for 10 minutes.

GARLICKY LAMB POT ROAST

Serves 8

- ☐ **3 cloves garlic, crushed**
- ☐ **1 teaspoon garam masala**
- ☐ **125 g (4 oz) fresh breadcrumbs**
- ☐ **2 tablespoons pine nuts**
- ☐ **1 tablespoon currants**
- ☐ **1 teaspoon grated lemon rind**
- ☐ **1.5 kg (3 lb) leg lamb, tunnel boned**
- ☐ **$^1/_2$ teaspoon ground nutmeg**
- ☐ **$^1/_2$ teaspoon ground cinnamon**
- ☐ **$^1/_2$ teaspoon ground black pepper**
- ☐ **2 tablespoons olive oil**
- ☐ **2 cups chicken stock**
- ☐ **2 tablespoons lemon juice**
- ☐ **250 g (8 oz) kumera, peeled, cut into julienne**
- ☐ **250 g (8 oz) green beans, topped and tailed**

1 Combine garlic, garam masala, breadcrumbs, pine nuts, currants and rind in a glass bowl. Spoon mixture into lamb cavity and secure with string. Combine nutmeg, cinnamon and pepper, rub over all surfaces of lamb.
2 Heat oil in large saucepan. Add meat and cook over high heat until browned. Add stock, cover and simmer over low heat for 25 minutes, turning occasionally. Mix in lemon juice, cover and simmer for 25 minutes longer. Add kumera and simmer for 5 minutes more. Remove lamb from pan and set aside and keep warm. Add beans and cook until tender. Season to taste. To serve, slice lamb and accompany with vegetables.

COOK'S TIP

To thicken pan juices, add 1 tablespoon cornflour blended with 60mL (2fl oz) water.

PORK RIBS WITH DIPPING SAUCE

Chopped into bite-sized pieces and stir-fried, these ribs are ideal to serve as a snack with drinks.

Serves 4

- ☐ **750 g (1$^1/_2$ lb) pork spare ribs**
- ☐ **2 cloves garlic, crushed**
- ☐ **1 teaspoon finely grated ginger**
- ☐ **1 tablespoon soy sauce**

DIPPING SAUCE
- ☐ **2 small red chillies, seeded, chopped finely**
- ☐ **1 shallot, chopped finely**
- ☐ **3 tablespoons brown sugar**
- ☐ **4 tablespoons brown vinegar**
- ☐ **1 tablespoon tamarind sauce**
- ☐ **3 tablespoons water**

1 To make sauce, combine chillies, shallot, sugar, vinegar, tamarind and water in a small bowl. Cover and set aside for 2 hours.
2 Combine ribs, garlic, ginger and soy sauce in a glass bowl. Cover and refrigerate for 2–4 hours or overnight. Grill, barbecue or stir-fry ribs over high heat until well browned. Serve with sauce.

Veal Cous Cous Casserole, Garlicky Lamb Pot Roast, Pork Ribs with Dipping Sauce

CHICKEN OMELETTE WITH CUCUMBER RELISH

Serves 4

- ☐ **2 tablespoons oil**
- ☐ **1 onion, peeled, chopped**
- ☐ **250 g (8 oz) minced chicken**
- ☐ **1 tomato, peeled, seeded, diced**
- ☐ **3 tablespoons frozen peas, thawed**
- ☐ **$^1/_2$ mango, mashed**
- ☐ **4 eggs, lightly beaten**
- ☐ **1 teaspoon finely chopped fresh mint**

CUCUMBER RELISH

- ☐ **2 tablespoons lime juice**
- ☐ **1 tablespoon chopped fresh mint**
- ☐ **1 cucumber, peeled and cut into thin strips**
- ☐ **1 small red chilli, seeded, finely chopped**
- ☐ **1 tablespoon sugar**
- ☐ **2 tablespoons soy sauce**
- ☐ **4 tablespoons water**

1   To make relish, combine lime juice, mint, cucumber, chilli, sugar, soy sauce and water in a bowl and cover until ready to serve. Strain liquid from relish before serving.

2   Heat 1 tablespoon oil in medium saucepan. Add onion and mince and cook over high heat for 5 minutes or until chicken is well browned. Stir in tomato and peas and cook, uncovered, stirring over low heat for 10 minutes. Remove from heat and stir in mango. Set aside and keep warm.

3   Heat remaining oil in 23 cm (9 in) omelette pan. Combine egg and mint mixture. Pour into pan and swirl mixture over base. Cook over moderate heat for about 3 minutes or until cooked, without turning. Slide omelette onto a paper lined board. Spread chicken mixture evenly over omelette. Using paper as a guide, roll up firmly like Swiss roll. To serve, slice omelette accompanied with relish.

❖

ORIENTAL PORK LETTUCE CUPS

Serves 4

- ☐ **4 dried Chinese mushrooms**
- ☐ **1 teaspoon sesame oil**
- ☐ **1 tablespoon peanut oil**
- ☐ **375 g (12 oz) pork fillet, cut into thin strips**
- ☐ **1 onion, peeled, sliced**
- ☐ **60 g (2 oz) mushrooms, sliced**
- ☐ **1 carrot, peeled, cut into thin julienne**
- ☐ **185 g (6 oz) bean sprouts**
- ☐ **1 clove garlic, crushed**
- ☐ **1 teaspoon grated fresh ginger**
- ☐ **2 teaspoons cornflour**
- ☐ **2 tablespoons oyster sauce**
- ☐ **2 tablespoons sweet sherry**
- ☐ **2 shallots, chopped**
- ☐ **8 small lettuce cups, washed, drained**

1   Place mushrooms in small bowl and cover with boiling water. Set aside for 20 minutes. Drain and slice thinly.

2   Heat sesame and peanut oils in wok or frypan. Add pork and cook over high heat for 5 minutes or until pork is browned. Add onion, mushrooms, carrot, sprouts, garlic and ginger and cook stirring over high heat for 2 minutes longer.

3   Combine cornflour, oyster sauce and sherry in pan. Cook, stirring until mixture boils and thickens. Stir in shallots. Remove from heat and spoon into lettuce cups. Serve immediately.

Chicken Omelette with Cucumber Relish, Oriental Pork Lettuce Cups

DRY FISH CURRY WITH ASPARAGUS

Serves 6

- ☐ **2 tablespoons oil**
- ☐ **1 clove garlic, crushed**
- ☐ **1 teaspoon brown mustard seeds**
- ☐ **3 tablespoons blanched whole almonds**
- ☐ **1 tablespoon curry paste**
- ☐ **1 tablespoon chopped fresh lemon grass**
- ☐ **750 g (1¹/₂ lb) boneless fish fillets, cut into strips**
- ☐ **4 tablespoons coconut cream**
- ☐ **410 g (13 oz) fresh asparagus, sliced into 5 cm (2in) pieces**

1   Heat oil in large frypan. Add garlic, mustard seeds and almonds and cook, stirring over medium heat for 4 minutes or until almonds are golden. Stir in paste and cook for 3 minutes longer.

2   Stir in lemon grass and fish and cook for 3–4 minutes or until fish is almost cooked. Add coconut cream and asparagus and cook stirring over high heat for 3 minutes. Season to taste and serve immediately.

❖

COCONUT VEGETABLE SKEWERS

These vegetable skewers make a great starter to any meal and are equally good as an accompaniment to a mild beef curry.

Serves 4

- ☐ **16 button mushrooms**
- ☐ **2 medium zucchini, chopped into 8 pieces**
- ☐ **8 whole baby onions, peeled**
- ☐ **16 cherry tomatoes**
- ☐ **125 g (4 oz) toasted shredded coconut**

MARINADE
- ☐ **1 tablespoon finely chopped fresh mint**
- ☐ **2 tablespoons lime juice**
- ☐ **2 teaspoons honey**
- ☐ **1 tablespoon sambal oelek**
- ☐ **4 tablespoons coconut cream**

1   To make marinade, combine mint, juice, honey, sambal oelek and coconut cream in a bowl. Add mushrooms, zucchini, onions and tomatoes, cover and set aside for 1 hour.

2   Drain off marinade and reserve. Thread vegetables alternately onto 8 bamboo skewers. Brush with reserved marinade and grill or barbecue over high heat for about 2 minutes. Brush with marinade and turn during cooking.

3   Remove skewers from heat, roll in coconut. Serve immediately.

Dry Fish Curry with Asparagus, Coconut Vegetable Skewers

Hot Pot Dinner Party

Intrigue your guests with this fun (and healthy!) way of cooking. The great entertainment advantage is that everyone will participate – so you can relax – and be assured that your guests will go away filled with admiration for your innovation ... and with second-helpings of this delicious food.

Chilli Hot Pot, Steamed Fish Bundles, Steamed Rice

MENU
Serves 12
◆
Chilli Hot Pot
◆
Steamed Fish Bundles
(double recipe)
◆
Steamed Rice
◆
Peach Buttermilk
Ice Cream

CHILLI HOT POT

Serve with hoisin sauce. For this recipe you will need 2 medium hotpots or 1 large.

Serves 12

- ☐ 1.2 L (2 pts) rich beef stock
- ☐ 1 teaspoon sesame oil
- ☐ 2 cloves garlic, crushed
- ☐ 2 teaspoons grated fresh ginger
- ☐ 3 small fresh red chillies, chopped
- ☐ 2 star anise
- ☐ 6 dried Chinese mushrooms
- ☐ 375 g (12 oz) rump steak, sliced thinly
- ☐ 2 tablespoons soy sauce
- ☐ 375 g (12 oz) pork and veal mince
- ☐ 1 teaspoon sesame seeds
- ☐ 1 tablespoon chilli sauce
- ☐ 1 egg, lightly beaten
- ☐ 125 mL (4 fl. oz) oil
- ☐ 375 g (12 oz) skinned chicken thigh fillets, sliced thinly
- ☐ 6 shallots, cut into 5 cm lengths
- ☐ 90 g (3 oz) bamboo shoots, sliced thinly
- ☐ 2 large carrots, sliced diagonally
- ☐ 1 red capsicum, sliced
- ☐ 1 cucumber, sliced
- ☐ 220 g (7 oz) Chinese cabbage, shredded
- ☐ 220 g (7 oz) egg noodles, cooked and drained

1   Combine stock, sesame oil, garlic, ginger, chillies and star anise in a large saucepan. Bring to the boil, reduce heat and simmer, covered for 5 minutes. Set aside and keep warm. Soak mushrooms in boiling water for 10 minutes. Drain and slice thinly. Combine steak and soy sauce in glass bowl and set aside.

2   Combine mince, seeds, sauce and egg in glass bowl, mix well. Shape mixture into small balls. Heat oil in frypan and cook balls until golden. Remove and drain on absorbent kitchen paper. Add chicken to same pan, cook over high heat until chicken is browned. Remove and drain on absorbent kitchen paper. Add beef to same pan and stir over high heat until browned. Remove and drain on absorbent kitchen paper.

3   Arrange beef, chicken, meatballs, vegetables and noodles attractively on a large platter. Pour warm stock into hotpot and heat gently over flame or coals. Using a small wire basket, each guest selects and cooks their own food in the boiling stock. At the end of the meal any remaining meat, vegetables or noodles are added to the stock and served as a soup.

❖

STEAMED FISH BUNDLES

Serves 6

- ☐ 6 small white fish fillets
- ☐ 1 teaspoon salt
- ☐ $1/2$ teaspoon ground saffron
- ☐ 1 onion, chopped
- ☐ 2 garlic cloves, sliced
- ☐ 2.5 cm (1 in) piece fresh ginger, sliced
- ☐ 1 small red chilli, seeded and chopped
- ☐ 1 tablespoon rice flour
- ☐ 185 mL (6 fl. oz) coconut cream
- ☐ 1 teaspoon sesame oil
- ☐ 1 stalk lemon grass, chopped
- ☐ 6 large lettuce leaves

1   Rub the fish well with half the salt and saffron and set aside.

2   Place onion, garlic, ginger, chilli, rice flour, coconut cream, sesame oil and lemon grass in a food processor or blender and process until smooth.

3   Steam, boil or microwave lettuce leaves until just soft. Drain and pat dry with absorbent paper. Top each lettuce leaf with a fish fillet. Spoon over a little onion puree and fold over lettuce leaf to seal.

4   Cut six foil squares large enough to enclose fish bundles. Place a bundle on each square and fold in edges to seal. Steam bundles for 20 minutes or until fish flakes when tested.

PEEL A PEACH

To peel peaches make a small cross at top using sharp knife. Place in a large bowl, pour over boiling water and allow to stand for 30 seconds. Rinse under cold water and peel away skin.

Delicious Hot Pot ingredients

PEACH BUTTERMILK ICE CREAM

Serves 6

- [ ] **8 medium peaches, peeled, halved and stones removed**
- [ ] **250 g (8 oz) sugar**
- [ ] **375 mL (12 fl. oz) buttermilk**
- [ ] **60 mL (2 fl. oz) Advocaat**
- [ ] **375 mL (12 fl. oz) cream**

1   Place peach halves and sugar in a food processor or blender and process until combined. Stir in buttermilk, Advocaat and cream.

2   Place ice cream mixture in a freezerproof container and freeze until completely frozen.

3   Remove from freezer, chop roughly, then beat with an electric mixer until smooth. Return to freezerproof container and refreeze.

Peach Buttermilk Ice Cream

HOT POT PARTIES

✧   A successful hot pot meal requires a little effort and preparation, but after that it's delicious food and great fun all the way.

✧   Ahead of time you can prepare as many dipping sauces as you like, such as sesame sauce, chilli sauce, soy sauce and so forth.

✧   When ready to start cooking, get some heat beads or charcoals to the white hot stage in your barbecue or hibachi. At the same time, start boiling up some chicken stock.

✧   Put down a thick chopping board, or similar, onto your table to protect it. When the charcoal or beads are ready, and the stock is boiling, put them down the spout of the hot pot (or fondue) then pour the boiling stock into the hot pot's 'moat'.

✧   Take very thinly sliced pieces of beef, chicken or other meat, fish parcels, sliced vegetables or whatever else you've prepared and drop them into the boiling stock. After they have simmered for a short time, take them out and serve.

✧   A Hot Pot Party can be uproarious – like the fondue parties of old, but involving far less risk to the waistline. Everybody will jostle for a position around the pot, everybody will forget what particular piece of food was theirs and everybody will enjoy finishing off the meal tucking into a bowl of the soup that's been made during the whole process.

✧   If your guests didn't know each other before the Hot Pot Party, they will be firm pals by its end.

✧   This type of party has the further advantage of being inexpensive. Even the equipment you need, such as throwaway wooden chopsticks, the pots themselves and the little wire strainers you need to extract your food, are cheaply available in any emporium of Asian food.

Cook Ahead Dinner Party

The fantastic advantage of the recipes in this book is that the foods' flavours, in almost every case, improve over time. You can, in fact, cook an entire dinner party ahead of time, refrigerate or freeze everything, and still be certain that quality and taste will not be diminished in the slightest. "Cheating" never made more sense!

Vegetable Soup, Athenian Lamb Hot Pot, Brussels Sprouts with Almonds, Country Style Cornbread

MENU
◆
Vegetable Soup
◆
Athenian Lamb Hot Pot
◆
Brussels Sprouts with
Almonds
◆
Country Style Cornbread
◆
Lime and Coconut
Baked Custard

Lime and Coconut Baked Custard

LIME AND COCONUT BAKED CUSTARD

Serves 6

- ☐ **3 eggs**
- ☐ **4 egg yolks**
- ☐ **185 g (6 oz) caster sugar**
- ☐ **375 mL (12 fl. oz) coconut milk**
- ☐ **125 mL (4 fl. oz) cream**
- ☐ **250 mL (8 fl. oz) milk**
- ☐ **375 g (12 oz) coconut**
- ☐ **2 tablespoons grated lime rind**
- ☐ **nutmeg for dusting**
- ☐ **toasted shredded coconut**
- ☐ **lime rind, extra for decoration**

1   Beat eggs, egg yolks and sugar in bowl until light and fluffy.

2   Combine coconut milk, cream and milk in a saucepan and heat until almost boiling. Remove from heat and set aside to cool slightly. Gradually pour milk into egg mixture and beat until combined. Mix in coconut and lime rind.

3   Pour custard into a buttered 500 mL (1 pint) ovenproof dish. Stand dish in baking pan, add boiling water to come halfway up the sides of the dish. Bake at 180°C (350°F) for 1 hour or until set.

4   Remove from oven and dust with nutmeg and decorate with coconut and lime. If desired serve with whipped cream.

COUNTRY STYLE CORNBREAD

Makes 1 loaf

- ☐ **6 bacon rashers, chopped**
- ☐ **6 shallots, finely chopped**
- ☐ **1 large green chilli, finely chopped**
- ☐ **60 g (2 oz) plain flour**
- ☐ **220 g (7 oz) cornmeal (polenta)**
- ☐ **1 tablespoon baking powder**
- ☐ **1 teaspoon salt**
- ☐ **2 eggs, lightly beaten**
- ☐ **375 mL (12 fl. oz) milk**
- ☐ **60 mL (2 fl. oz) maize oil**
- ☐ **125 g (4 oz) unflavoured yoghurt**
- ☐ **250 g (8 oz) canned creamed corn**
- ☐ **125 g (4 oz) grated tasty cheese**
- ☐ **freshly ground pepper**

1   Cook bacon and shallots in a non stick frypan for 2–3 minutes or until bacon is crisp. Add chilli to pan and cook for 1 minute longer.

2   Sift together flour, cornmeal, baking powder and salt. Combine eggs, milk, oil, yoghurt, corn, cheese and pepper in a large mixing bowl. Add bacon mixture, then fold in sifted dry ingredients.

3   Spoon mixture into a well greased 25 cm (10 in) flan pan. Bake at 180°C (350°F) for 1$\frac{1}{4}$ hours or until golden. Cool in pan for 10 minutes before turning out.

VEGETABLE SOUP

A hearty vegetable soup that is also great served with crusty bread for lunch and is sure to keep winter chills at bay.

Serves 6

- ☐ 1 tablespoon olive oil
- ☐ 1 leek, finely sliced
- ☐ 1 clove garlic, crushed
- ☐ 1 stick celery, chopped
- ☐ 1 large carrot, diced
- ☐ 440 g (14 oz) canned, peeled tomatoes, drained and mashed
- ☐ 2 tablespoons tomato puree
- ☐ 1.5 L (2¹/₂ pts) chicken stock
- ☐ 1 large potato, diced
- ☐ 60 g (2 oz) shelled peas
- ☐ freshly ground black pepper
- ☐ 1 teaspoon finely chopped fresh basil
- ☐ 1 tablespoon finely chopped fresh parsley
- ☐ 1 tablespoon finely chopped chives
- ☐ 2 tablespoons freshly grated Parmesan cheese

1   In a large saucepan, heat oil, cook leek and garlic for 5 minutes or until leek softens. Add celery and carrot, cook for 5 minutes longer.
2   Stir in tomatoes, tomato puree and stock, bring to the boil, reduce heat and simmer for 10 minutes.
3   Add potato and peas and cook for 10 minutes longer or until potato is tender. Season to taste with pepper. Just before serving, stir in basil, parsley and chives and sprinkle with Parmesan cheese.

ATHENIAN LAMB HOT POT

Serves 6

- ☐ 1 kg (2 lb) boneless lamb, cubed
- ☐ 3 tablespoons olive oil
- ☐ 2 onions, finely chopped
- ☐ 1 green capsicum, seeded and chopped
- ☐ 250 mL (8 fl. oz) tomato paste
- ☐ 185 mL (6 fl. oz) chicken stock
- ☐ ¹/₂ teaspoon ground cardamom
- ☐ 1 large cinnamon stick
- ☐ freshly ground black pepper
- ☐ 2 tablespoons chopped fresh coriander

1   Trim meat of all visible fat. Heat 2 tablespoons of oil in a large saucepan. Cook the meat in batches until well browned on all sides. Transfer to a plate and set aside.
2   Heat remaining oil and cook onion and capsicum for 2–3 minutes or until onion softens. Stir in tomato paste and stock. Stir well to lift pan sediment.
3   Add cardamom, cinnamon and pepper. Bring to the boil, reduce heat and simmer for 5 minutes. Return meat to the pan with coriander. Cover and simmer for 1¹/₂ hours or until meat is tender and sauce thickens.

BRUSSELS SPROUTS WITH ALMONDS

Serves 6

- ☐ 750 g (1¹/₂ lbs) Brussels sprouts
- ☐ 3 tablespoons flaked almonds

SAUCE
- ☐ 30 g butter, melted
- ☐ 2 tablespoons brown sugar
- ☐ 3 teaspoons cornflour
- ☐ ¹/₂ teaspoon prepared mustard
- ☐ 1 small onion, finely chopped
- ☐ 3 tablespoons white vinegar

1   Boil, steam or microwave Brussels sprouts until tender. Drain and keep warm.
2   Combine butter, sugar, cornflour, mustard, onion and vinegar in a saucepan. Cook, stirring until sauce boils and thickens. Pour over Brussels sprouts and top with toasted almonds.

Fresh Bread

Our selection of bread recipes will change the way you look at the 'staff of life' With our help you'll make absolutely delicious sesame buns, chapatis, rotis and pita breads. If you're not yet familiar with some of these, you're in for a great treat.

CHAPATIS

An Indian unleavened bread that is eaten with all curries and savoury dishes. Break off a piece of bread and use it to scoop up the food. Chapatis should be served warm.

Makes 12–14

- ☐ **280 g (9 oz) wholemeal flour, sifted**
- ☐ **125–155 mL (4–5 fl. oz) warm water**
- ☐ **15 g (^{1}/2 oz) ghee**

1   Place flour in a mixing bowl and work in enough water to form a firm dough. Knead for 8 minutes or until dough is soft and elastic. Cover and stand for 1 hour.
2   Divide dough into 12 portions. On a lightly floured surface, roll each portion of dough to a 13 cm (5 in) round.
3   Heat a heavy-based frypan and grease lightly with ghee. Cook the chapatis over a medium heat until brown flecks appear on the surface. Turn and press with a ghee moistened cloth to encourage it to bubble. Note: the more the dough is kneaded the lighter and more elastic it will be.

COOK'S TIP

✦   The protein content and age of the flour affects the absorption of the water and sometimes you will find that extra water may be required to achieve the right consistency for a bread dough.
✦   Salt is an important ingredient in bread making, while it is not essential the lack of it is very noticeable. Too little salt tends to leave the bread tasting flat and the dough feeling slack during kneading. Too much salt however makes the bread taste bitter and will slow the yeast activity.

ROTIS

These are Sri Lankan flat-style breads that are best eaten warm.

Makes 12

- ☐ **250 g (8 oz) self-raising flour**
- ☐ **90 g (3 oz) rice flour**
- ☐ **60 g (2 oz) desiccated coconut**
- ☐ **1 teaspoon salt**
- ☐ **315 mL (10 fl. oz) cold water**
- ☐ **15 g (^{1}/2 oz) ghee**

1   Sift self-raising and rice flours together into a bowl. Add coconut and salt, mix well to combine.
2   Make a well in the centre of the dry ingredients and add most of the water. Mix to a dough and add remaining water if necessary. Knead until smooth and soft. Cover and allow to stand for 40 minutes.
3   Divide dough into 12 portions and flatten into rounds. Heat a heavy-based frypan until hot. Spread each side of the dough rounds with a little ghee. Cook until golden on both sides, turning half way through cooking.

SESAME BUNS

These buns are hollow in the centre when baked. Cut them in half to serve and the pocket can be filled with a tasty recipe of your choice.

Makes 12

- ☐ **75 mL (2^1/2 fl. oz) vegetable oil**
- ☐ **625 g (1^1/4 lb) plain flour**
- ☐ **315 mL (10 fl. oz) boiling water**
- ☐ **2 teaspoons salt**
- ☐ **3 teaspoons sesame seeds**

1   Heat oil in a frypan, add 125 g (4 oz) of flour and cook until light and golden in colour. Remove from heat and set aside to cool. Sift remaining flour into a bowl and add water. Mix quickly to form a dough, cover and set aside to stand for 5 minutes.
2   Turn dough onto a lightly oiled surface and knead for 7 minutes or until dough is smooth and pliable. Divide into 12 pieces. Roll each piece into a square and spread one side with the cooked flour paste. Roll the dough out a little larger, moisten the smooth side with a little water and sprinkle with sesame seeds.
3   Place buns on lightly greased baking trays and bake at 200°C (400°F) for 7 minutes. Turn buns over and bake for a further 7 minutes or until crisp and puffed.

FRENCH PLAIT

This attractive European style bread is ideal to serve with soups. The dough can be used to make any shaped loaf that you like.

- ☐ **15 g (1/2 oz) fresh yeast**
- ☐ **440 mL (14 fl.oz) warm water**
- ☐ **750 g (1 1/2 lb) white flour**
- ☐ **2 teaspoons salt**
- ☐ **1 teaspoon sugar**
- ☐ **15 g (1/2 oz) butter**
- ☐ **1 egg, lightly beaten**
- ☐ **2 tablespoons sesame seeds**

1   Blend yeast with water and whisk with a fork until yeast dissolves.
2   Place flour, salt and sugar in a bowl, add butter and rub in with fingers. Make a well in the centre of the dry ingredients and add the yeast mixture, mix with a wooden spoon to form a soft dough. Knead with hands until dough leaves the sides of the bowl.
3   Turn dough out onto a lightly floured board and knead for 10 minutes or until dough is elastic and no longer sticky. Shape dough into a ball and place in an oiled bowl, cover and set aside in a warm place for 1 hour or until doubled in size.
4   Divide dough into three equal portions and shape each portion into a thin roll 30 cm (12 in) long. Dampen ends of each roll and join together at one end and plait loosely. Place on a lightly greased baking tray, cover and set aside in a warm place until doubled in size.
5   Brush loaf with egg and sprinkle with sesame seeds. Cook at 220°C (425°F) for 25–30 minutes or until golden and well risen.

PITA BREAD

You can bake you own pita bread and enjoy it when it is still warm and puffed. As the bread is cooked, wrap it in a cloth to keep soft and warm.

Makes 12

- ☐ **500 g (1 lb) wholemeal flour**
- ☐ **1 teaspoon salt**
- ☐ **7¹/₂ g (¹/₄ oz) dry yeast**
- ☐ **2 teaspoons sugar**
- ☐ **375 mL (12 fl. oz) warm water**

1   Sift flour and salt together. Measure out 125 g (4 oz) flour and reserve. Dissolve yeast and sugar in water and set aside.
2   Make a well in the centre of the flour and add the yeast mixture. Mix in a little of the flour from the sides to form a thick liquid, cover and set aside in a warm place until frothy. Draw in remaining flour and mix to form a dough. Knead dough using some of the reserved flour, for 5–10 minutes or until smooth. Shape into a ball and sprinkle lightly with flour. Place in a lightly greased bowl, cover and set aside in a warm place, until doubled in bulk.
3   Punch dough down, turn out on a lightly floured surface and knead for 1 minute. Divide into 12 portions and shape each portion into a ball. Cover and set aside in a warm place until doubled in bulk.
4   Roll each dough ball to a 15 cm (6 in) round and place on a lightly floured tea towel. Cover and set aside for 20 minutes.
5   Place baking trays in oven and heat at 260°C for 10 minutes, before lightly greasing. Carefully lift two rounds onto each baking tray and cook for 4 minutes or until pita puffs. Turn pita and cook for a further 4 minutes. Remove from oven and wrap in a cloth to keep soft and warm. Repeat until all pita rounds are cooked.

HIGH RISE

There are two types of yeast that are commonly used in breadmaking – fresh and dried.

✦   Dried yeast works just as well as fresh but takes longer to activate. As it is twice as concentrated as fresh yeast only half as much is needed. 15 g (1/2 oz) dried yeast has the same raising power as 30 g (1 oz) fresh yeast.

✦   Fresh yeast will keep in a loosely tied polythene bag in the refrigerator for about a week.

✦   Dried yeast will keep in a cool dark place for about six months. Yeast will deteriorate if exposed to air.

✦   Yeast works best in warm conditions. Cold and draughts slow down its growth, whereas an intense heat will kill it.

✦   The amount of yeast required depends on the richness of the dough. The more sugar and fat there is in a dough, the more yeast it needs to raise it.

✦   Using too much yeast will give a crumbly, sour tasting bread which will go stale quickly.

✦   Fresh yeast works best when mixed with liquid that is at about 25°C (78°F) and dried yeast at 40°C (104°F).

✦   An easy way of making sure that the liquid is at the right temperature is to bring one-third of it to the boil and add the rest cold.

Meat Know-How

Knowing a little about meat will help you understand why we grill a sirloin steak but casserole blade steak. Where the meat comes from on an animal determines how you are going to cook it. The tenderest cuts are from those areas that are the least exercised. The less tender cuts come from areas such as the shoulder or leg, which are in constant use, whenever the animal moves. This guide to meat cuts and cooking techniques will help you to understand meat better and know how to cook it.

COOKING METHODS

Cooking methods can be divided into groups – dry heat and moist heat methods.

DRY HEAT METHODS

Pan-fry
Suitable cuts
Beef: blade, gillet, round (minute), rump, rib eye, spare ribs, sirloin/T-bone, silverside (sandwich) steak
Lamb: best neck chops and cutlets, chump, leg and mid loin chops, loin chops and cutlets
Veal: leg steak, loin chops, cutlets

Stir-Fry
Suitable cuts
Beef: blade, fillet, round, rump, rib eye, topside, sirloin steak
Lamb: boneless lamb, boneless shoulder, boneless mid loin, fillet

Crumb-Fry
Suitable cuts
Beef: blade, round (minute), topside steak
Lamb: best neck chops, rib loin cutlets
Veal: leg steaks, schnitzel, loin chops, cutlets

Grill
Suitable cuts
Beef: blade, fillet, rump, rib eye, spare ribs, sirloin/T-bone, silverside (sandwich) steak
Lamb: best neck chops and cutlets, chump, forequarter, leg and mid loin chops, rib loin chops and cutlets, shoulder chops
Veal: leg steak, loin chops and cutlets

Barbecue
Suitable cuts
Beef: blade, fillet, rump, rib eye, spare ribs, sirloin/T-bone steak
Lamb: chump, forequarter, leg, shoulder and mid loin chops, rib loin chops and cutlets
Veal: leg steak, loin chops and cutlets

Oven Roast
Suitable cuts
Beef: blade, fillet, rump, rib roast, spare ribs, sirloin, fresh silverside, topside

Lamb: breast, chump, forequarter, leg, mid loin, rib loin, rack, crown roast, shank, shoulder
Veal: leg, loin, rack, shoulder/forequarter

MOIST HEAT METHODS

Pot Roast
Suitable cuts
Beef: blade, brisket, chuck, round, fresh silverside, skirt, topside
Lamb: forequarter, shank, shoulder
Veal: shoulder/forequarter

Casserole
Suitable cuts
Beef: blade, brisket, chuck, round, spare ribs, shin, fresh silverside, skirt, topside
Lamb: best neck, forequarter, neck chops, cracked shanks, shoulder chops
Veal: shoulder/forequarter chops and steaks, neck chops, knuckle

Braise
Suitable cuts
Beef: blade, brisket, chuck, round, spare ribs, shin, fresh silverside, skirt, topside
Lamb: best neck, forequarter, neck chops, cracked shank, shoulder chops
Veal: shoulder/forequarter chops and steaks, neck chops, knuckle

Stew
Suitable cuts
Beef: blade, brisket, chuck, round, spare ribs, shin, fresh silverside, skirt, topside
Lamb: best neck, forequarter/shoulder and neck chops, cracked shank
Veal: forequarter/shoulder chops and steaks, neck chops, knuckle

Simmer
Suitable cuts
Beef: corned silverside, corned brisket

Basic Lamb Cuts

1 Leg
leg roast
leg chops
fillet of leg

2 Chump
chump chops

3 Fillet

4 Eye of Loin

5 Mid loin/loin
mid loin chops
boneless loin roast

6 Rib/best end of neck
cutlets
rack
crown roast

7 Forequarter/shoulder
forequarter chops
shoulder roast (bone in)
boneless shoulder roast

8 Neck
neck rosettes
best neck chops

9 Shank/knuckle

10 Breast

Basic Beef Cuts

1 Shin
shin bone-in
boneless shin

2 Silverside/topside
silverside steak
silverside roast
topside steak
topside roast

3 Round
round steak
thick flank

4 Rump
rump steak
rump roast

5 Fillet
fillet steak

6 Skirt/flank
flank steak

7 Sirloin
boneless sirloin steak
sirloin steak bone-in
t-bone steak
sirloin roast
porterhouse steak

8 Ribs
rib steak
rib eye
rib eye steaks
rolled rib roast

9 Blade/chuck/neck
chuck steak
chuck pot roast
blade steak
oyster blade steak
shoulder cut
neck

10 Brisket/plate
short ribs
brisket (corned beef)

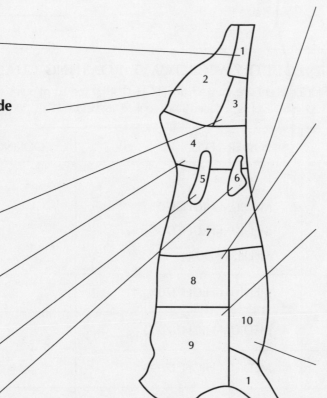

MICROWAVING MEAT

Cooking meat in the microwave is straight forward as long as you remember a few simple rules. Many of the recipes in this book could be microwaved, with only minor changes. Recipes that lend themselves to microwaving are the longer cooking dishes. Shorter cooking dishes such as stir-fries are generally not worth microwaving. The following guide will enable you to adapt many of the recipes for the microwave.

Microwave Roasting

✧ Elevate meat on a roasting rack to ensure even cooking.

✧ Turn roasts once or twice during cooking, to ensure the roast cooks evenly.

✧ Check meat half way through cooking and if outer edges are cooked, shield with foil. Do not allow foil to touch the sides of the microwave and make sure that at least half the food is exposed to microwave energy.

✧ To achieve a roast effect, cook uncovered.

✧ Do not salt meat as this will toughen the outside.

✧ To achieve a pot roast effect, cook meat in an oven bag.

✧ When cooking a crown roast or a rack of lamb cover the tips of the bones with foil.

✧ Allow meat to stand for 10–15 minutes before carving. Wrap roast in foil for standing.

✧ Allowing meat to stand on completion of cooking ensures that the meat is completely cooked, as the temperature rises slightly during this time. Standing also allows the juices in the meat to settle and makes carving easier.

Microwave casseroles

✧ Smaller casseroles, up to 1 kg (2 lb) of meat, are most suitable for microwave cooking.

✧ The less tender cuts of meat used in casseroles require longer, slower cooking as in conventional cooking.

✧ A casserole using 500 g (1 lb) of beef will take 45 minutes to an hour to cook.

✧ The smaller the meat is cut, the shorter the cooking time.

✧ Cut meat and vegetables about the same size.

✧ Use less liquid when cooking casseroles in the microwave.

✧ A casserole cooked the day before it is required and then refrigerated will have more flavour than a freshly cooked casserole. Standing allows the flavour to develop.

✧ When making curries in the microwave, cook the first stage in the traditional way – cook the onions and spices in the frypan, then place everything in a casserole dish. Cook as for casseroles and the wonderful flavours we all associate with curries will be retained.

EASY CASSEROLE

When cooking a casserole in the microwave, dice 500 g (1 lb) beef. Place meat, 2 tablespoons flour and any seasonings in a bag and toss to coat the meat with flour. Place in 2L (3^1/2 pts) casserole dish with chopped vegetables and 600 mL (1 pt) liquid. The liquid should just cover the meat. Cover casserole and cook on HIGH (100%) for 10 minutes, reduce power level to MEDIUM (50%) and cook for 45 minutes longer.

MEAT AND POULTRY MICROWAVE ROASTING CHART

All roasts (except for chicken) are cooked on HIGH (100%) for 10 minutes then the power level is reduced and cooked as below.

FOOD	POWER LEVEL	COOKING TIME PER 500 G (lb)
Beef		
Well-done	MEDIUM-HIGH (70%)	10 minutes
Medium	MEDIUM-HIGH (70%)	9 minutes
Rare	MEDIUM (50%)	10 minutes
Lamb	MEDIUM-HIGH (70%)	10 minutes
Pork	MEDIUM-HIGH (70%)	14 minutes
Turkey	MEDIUM-HIGH (70%)	10 minutes
Chicken	HIGH (100%)	10 minutes

MICROWAVING POULTRY

Microwaved poultry is tender and juicy and with the help of bastes and browners looks attractive and appetising.

✧ Commercial browners are available or you can make up your own mixes. A popular baste for poultry is a mixture made of 1 tablespoon soy sauce, 2 tablespoons tomato sauce and a little ground ginger.

✧ A baste of honey, lemon juice and soy sauce is also a delicious addition to roast poultry.

✧ When roasting poultry, tie legs of bird together or they will spread during cooking and overcook. To prevent wings from overcooking, tuck under the bird.

✧ Stand bird wrapped in foil for 10 minutes before serving.

✧ If stuffing a bird you will need to add 2 minutes to the total cooking time to ensure the stuffing and bird are cooked through.

MEAT PURCHASING GUIDE

When purchasing meat, the following tips will ensure that you purchase the best quality.

✧ Allow 125 g (4 oz) – 150 g (5 oz) lean boneless meat per serve.

✧ Meat should be bright red in colour with a fresh appearance.

✧ Select lean meat, if there is any fat it should be pale cream in colour.

✧ In hot climates, take an insulated shopping bag with you to ensure meat remains cold until you get it home and refrigerate it.

✧ When purchasing 'special cuts' ring your butcher and order in advance. In most cases if you give the butcher one to two days warning he will be able to supply you with any special cuts you may require.

MEAT STORAGE GUIDE

The following tips will ensure that the meat you purchase stays at its best for the longest possible time.

✧ Fresh meat should be kept as dry as possible and should not sit in its own 'drip' during storage.

✧ Store meat in the coldest part of the refrigerator. This will be the bottom shelf if your refrigerator does not have a special meat compartment.

✧ The more cutting and preparation meat has had, the shorter the storage time, for example mince has a shorter storage time than chops or steak.

✧ When storing meat in the refrigerator, place a stainless steel or plastic rack in a dish deep enough to catch any drip from the meat. Unwrap the meat and place on the rack in stacks of not more than three layers. Cover loosely with foil or waxed paper.

✧ If your refrigerator has a special meat storage compartment, unwrap the meat, arrange in stacks of not more than three layers and cover meat loosely with foil or waxed paper.

✧ If meat is to be used within two days of purchase, it can be left in its original wrapping. Store the package in the special meat compartment or the coldest part of the refrigerator.

✧ Meat that has been kept in the refrigerator for two or three days will be more tender than meat cooked on the day of purchase. Because of the natural enzymes softening the muscle fibres.

QUICK STORAGE GUIDE	
Mince and sausages	2 days
Cubed beef and lamb	3 days
Steaks, chops and cutlets	4 days
Roasting joints (with bone in)	3 to 5 days
Roasting joints (boned and rolled)	2 to 3 days
Corned beef	7 days

MEAT NUTRITION

Lean meat plays an important part in a balanced diet.

✧ A 'balanced' diet is one which has a balance of the five food groups. The complex carbohydrates, fibre, vitamins and minerals form bread, cereals and other grain foods, fruit and vegetables; the high protein and calcium of dairy products, with very little added fat all help to create that balanced diet.

✧ Lean beef and lamb are highly nutritious. A 125 g (4 oz) cooked serve provides much of the daily requirement of protein, the B-group vitamins, iron and zinc.

Taking Stock

You don't have to be a gourmet to know that many classic dishes rely on their stock for a rich, flavoursome base. Stocks play a crucial role in the cooking of casseroles and curries. Our traditional, time-honoured recipes and methods for white and brown stocks will always stand you in good stead; for that special seafood dish try our easy vegetable or fish stock.

TYPES OF STOCK

There are many different types of stock and stock can be made from almost any ingredients. However all stocks are either white or brown.

A white stock is made by putting all the ingredients in a pot and pouring over cold water. The stock is then brought to the boil and simmered for several hours.

A brown stock is made by first cooking the bones either in an oven or frypan until the fat runs, for 15–30 minutes. The vegetables are then added and cooked for 30 minutes longer. Drain off fat and place bones and vegetables in a pot, pour over cold water and add any flavourings you wish. Bring to the boil and simmer for several hours.

No matter which type of stock you make, during cooking skim any scum from the surface and once the stock is cooked, cool as quickly as possible then skim the fat off the top. The stock can now be refrigerated or frozen and used as required.

KEEPING STOCK

Stock will keep in the refrigerator for 3–4 days or in the freezer for 12 months. As stock really does not keep very well, except in the freezer it is better to freeze even if you are only keeping it for a few days.

Freeze It

Freeze stock in 125 mL (4 fl.oz) or 250 mL (8 fl.oz) portions for easy use at a later date. It is also a good idea to freeze some stock in ice cube trays for those times when you only require one or two tablespoons of stock. Remember, once the stock is frozen, to remove it from the trays and place in a freezer bag or it will evaporate and you will be left with nothing. Once stock has been frozen in the trays, they are no longer suitable for ice as the stock taints the tray and the flavour will be absorbed by the ice cubes.

STOCK INGREDIENTS

The main ingredients will depend on the type of stock you wish to make and can be almost anything you wish. The essential ingredients however are onions, carrots, celery and some herbs – fresh if possible. The ingredients should be roughly chopped to extract as much flavour as possible during cooking. The longer you cook a stock the more concentrated the flavour will be.

Bones

Beef, veal and poultry bones are best for a basic meat stock but other bones can be used when available or for a particular flavour. The more meat there is on the bones the better the stock will be. As bones contain gelatine this gives a slight body to the stock and if concentrated the stock will set. Raw veal bones and chicken feet contain the most gelatine.

Pork bones make a rather sweet stock. If using pork bones, combine them with veal bones for a more balanced stock. Lamb and ham bones make a very strong stock and ham bones a salty stock if the stock is concentrated too much.

Bones to be used in stock should be cut into chunks so as much flavour as possible is extracted during the cooking. If buying raw bones, ask your butcher to cut them.

Any scraps of meat will also add a good flavour to your stock, but they should be trimmed of fat.

Vegetables

Carrots, onions, celery and leeks are the most popular stock vegetables. Vegetables such as turnip, cauliflower and leafy green vegetables tend to have too strong a flavour to use in stock. However parsnips and over-ripe tomatoes are an excellent addition to the stock pot.

Herbs and Spices

Bay leaves, thyme and parsley are the most popular stock herbs. Include parsley stalks as well as the leaves. Use peppercorns for seasoning but not salt.

VEGETABLE STOCK

The best vegetable stock ever – well worth the effort to make. It will add a delicious flavour to any soup or casserole and is a must for any vegetarian.

Makes 2 L (3$^{1}/_{4}$ pts)

☐ **2 large onions, quartered**
☐ **2 large carrots, roughly chopped**
☐ **1 head celery, leaves included, roughly chopped**
☐ **1 large bunch parsley, stalks included, roughly chopped**
☐ **$^{1}/_{2}$ teaspoon black peppercorns**
☐ **2.5 L (4$^{1}/_{4}$ pts) cold water**

1   Place onions, carrots, celery, parsley, peppercorns and water in a large pot. Bring to the boil, reduce heat and simmer for 30 minutes, stirring occasionally.
2   Remove from heat and allow to cool.
3   Puree cold vegetable mixture, then push through a sieve. Use as required.

BEEF STOCK

This recipe will make a rich stock. If you wish the meat can be omitted and just the bones used.

Makes 2 L (3$^{1}/_{4}$ pts)

☐ **500 g (1lb) shin beef, diced**
☐ **500 g (1lb) marrow bones, cut into pieces**
☐ **1 onion, quartered**
☐ **2 carrots, roughly chopped**
☐ **4 stalks celery, roughly chopped**
☐ **fresh herbs of your choice**
☐ **4 peppercorns**
☐ **3 L (5 pts) cold water**

1   Place beef, bones, onion, carrots, celery, herbs, peppercorns and water in a large pot. Bring to the boil, reduce heat and simmer for 2 hours, stirring occasionally.
2   Strain stock and refrigerate overnight.
3   Skim fat from the surface and use as required.

WATCHPOINT

Do not add salt to stock when making it. Especially if you do not know how it is to be used. Salting stock can lead to an over-salty dish, if you reduce the stock or if using with ham.

FISH STOCK

Makes 2 L (3$^{1}/_{4}$ pts)

Fish stock is even better if you can include the shells of lobster, prawns or crab in it. When making fish stock it is important that the cooking time is no longer than 20 minutes as the bones and trimmings become bitter and impart an unpleasant taste.

☐ **fish bones, skins and seafood shells, the quantity and type used is not important**
☐ **1 large onion, quartered**
☐ **1 large carrot, roughly chopped**
☐ **4 stalks celery, roughly chopped**
☐ **1 bay leaf**
☐ **1 sprig fresh thyme**
☐ **$^{1}/_{2}$ teaspoon black peppercorns**
☐ **3 L (5 pts) cold water**

1   Place fish trimmings, onion, carrot, celery, bay leaf, thyme, peppercorns and water in a large pot. Bring to the boil, reduce heat and simmer for 20 minutes.
2   Strain stock and use as required.

CHICKEN STOCK

Makes 2 L (3$^{1}/_{4}$ pts)

☐ **1 chicken carcass, skin removed and trimmed of all visible fat**
☐ **1 onion, quartered**
☐ **2 carrots, roughly chopped**
☐ **4 stalks celery, roughly chopped**
☐ **fresh herbs of your choice**
☐ **$^{1}/_{2}$ teaspoon black peppercorns**
☐ **3 L (5 pts) cold water**

1   Place chicken carcass, onion, carrots, celery, herbs, peppercorns and water in a large pot. Bring to the boil, reduce heat and simmer for 2 hours, stirring occasionally.
2   Strain stock and refrigerate overnight.
3   Skim fat from the surface and use as required.

MICROWAVE STOCK

The microwave is particularly good for making small quantities of stock. The chicken carcass remaining after a roast is ideal for making stock. To make chicken stock in the microwave, place chicken carcass, 1 chopped onion, 1 chopped carrot and 2 stalks chopped celery, parsley and thyme in a large microwave-safe container. Add water to cover ingredients. Cook, uncovered on HIGH (100%) for 45 minutes.   Beef, fish and vegetable stock can be made in much the same way. Beef stock requires a little longer cooking and fish stock should not be cooked for more than 20 minutes.

Freezer Know-How

Whether you have a large free-standing freezer or just an icebox at the top of your fridge, make the most of it! Conjure up the summer smells and tastes in midwinter, and make the most of flavours that just love a chance to combine properly at the same time! Our wily ways with freezing will help you utilise your space economically by storing delicious pastes and bases for soups, casseroles and curries for quick and convenient use.

FREEZING RULES

One of the most important things to consider when freezing is the wrapping or containers used for the frozen food. Wrappings should be nonporous so that flavours and odours cannot escape from the food or other odours enter the food. Wrappings should be strong, have no taste or odour of their own and be moisture-proof. For best results, as much air as possible should be removed from the container holding the food before freezing. Air discolours food and causes dehydration, also known as freezer-burn. Dehydration dramatically affects the quality of the food and will make a juicy red steak tough, grey and tasteless. Should dehydration occur the food should be thrown away, as there is no way that quality can be restored.

Dehydration is a direct result of poor or incorrect packaging.

While as much air as possible should be removed from containers before freezing, those foods containing large quantities of liquid or all liquid such as soups and sauces require head space as the liquid expands on freezing. Allow 1–2 cm ($^1/_2$–1 in) head space for containers of 600 mL–1.2 litres (1–2 pints). If this head space is not allowed, tops can blow off containers with the contents all over the freezer.

Always label the food as you pack it with date and contents. Frozen food looks very different from fresh food and in a week, month or year you may not know what is in the packet or how long it has been there.

FREEZER GUIDE

While food can be kept for longer than the times given below, the following storage times will ensure that the food stays at its' best.

Food	Freezer Storage Life
Beef	12 months
Lamb	9 months
Pork	6 months
Veal	9 months
Ham on the bone	3 months
Ham, sliced	1 month
Bacon, sliced	1 month
Chicken	12 months
Turkey	6 months
Duck	6 months
Oily fish such as salmon, trout, mackerel	2 months
White fish	6 months
Shellfish	1 month
Casseroles	6 months
Curries	6 months
Soups	6–12 months
Stock	6–12 months

FREEZING SPICY DISHES

Have you ever wondered why casseroles, curries and other spicy foods seem to taste different after they have been frozen or left in the fridge overnight?

One reason is that the oils from the herbs and spices used to flavour these dishes 'bleed' until their essence has permeated through the food. Freezing gives seasonings more time to blend with food, so you will often find that the dish will taste more strongly seasoned when reheated. Remember if you are cooking food to freeze, especially spicy or hot dishes, it may be better to under-season them slightly. If necessary, the seasonings can be corrected during reheating – it is easier to add more spicy flavour than to take it away.

Another reason for the intensifying in flavour of reheated food is that moisture content reduces and so concentrates flavour.

Storing Spices

Storing ground spices in the freezer ensures stronger, more aromatic flavours. Commercially ground spices lose their flavour and aroma quickly. You can expect them to be at their best for up to six months after purchase. Grinding causes the surface area to increase considerably and therefore exposes the spices to oxygen, which leads to flavour loss.

FREEZING HERBS

If you grow your own herbs, use the freezer to preserve them. Frozen herbs are closest in flavour and colour to fresh herbs, they are ideal to use in cooking. Herbs that freeze particularly well are chervil, chives, dill, fennel leaves, parsley and tarragon.

The changes that take place during freezing have to do with appearance and texture rather than flavour. Leafy herbs tend to go limp, darken and toughen slightly, so, while not suitable for garnishing, they are perfect to use in cooking. Use the same quantity of frozen herbs as you would fresh in cooking. There is no need to thaw, just add straight to the recipe.

Preparation

There are several ways of freezing herbs, the simplest is to collect them in the early morning after the dew has dried. Wash the herbs gently under cold running water and shake off excess water. Place on absorbent kitchen paper and pat dry. Place in a freezer bag and freeze.

Blanching

Some herbs are better if blanched before freezing because blanching concentrates the flavours. Blanched herbs should be used in the same quantities as you would use dried herbs, so if a recipe calls for fresh herbs and you only have dried or blanched frozen herbs, use only half the quantity specified.

To prepare herbs for freezing by blanching, bring a pot of water to the boil and, using tongs, dip stalks of herbs into the water for a few seconds. Place on absorbent kitchen paper and allow to cool. Place in freezer bags and freeze. Basil and thyme are two herbs that are better if blanched before freezing. With most other herbs there seems to be no advantage to blanching, unless you wish to keep them for longer than six months in which case blanching will improve the quality of the frozen herbs considerably.

Ways of Freezing

Herbs can be frozen in a number of ways, on the stem, single leaves, sprigs, diced or chopped. Stems, sprigs and leaves are best if tray frozen first. They do not stick together during freezing and are easy to use and remove for cooking. After preparation, place the herbs on a tray lined with foil or freezer wrap and freeze overnight, then pack into freezer bags or containers.

Diced or chopped herbs can be frozen in two ways. Place the diced or chopped herbs straight into a freezer bag and freeze, then, when needed, scoop out the required amount.

Alternatively, place the chopped or diced herbs in an ice cube tray with a little stock or water and freeze. When frozen, remove from tray and pack into freezer bags. Just add to the pot for instant flavour when required.

You might like to consider freezing favourite combinations of herbs in ice cube form, so that only one or two cubes need to be added – make sure you know which is which by labelling them. Another way to preserve herbs is to freeze them in butter or oil.

FROZEN PESTO SAUCE

This tasty and traditional accompaniment to all types of pasta, is a particularly useful way of preserving basil and has a multitude of uses.

Makes 1 cup

- [ ] **3 cloves garlic**
- [ ] **125 g (4 oz) fresh basil leaves**
- [ ] **2 tablespoons chopped pine-nuts**
- [ ] **30 g grated Parmesan cheese**
- [ ] **185 mL (6 fl.oz) olive oil**

1 Place garlic in food processor or blender and puree. Scrape down any garlic from sides. Add basil leaves, and using pulse button, process until finely chopped.
2 Add nuts and cheese, and using pulse button, process until finely chopped and mixture is combined.
3 With food processor or blender running, add oil a tablespoon at a time until sauce is the consistency of thick soup.
4 To freeze, pack pesto in small portions and freeze. Use as a sauce on pasta and vegetables. Pesto sauce also makes a tasty addition to a casserole when stirred in just before serving.

FREEZING SOUPS

Soups are the ideal food to freeze. Make nourishing soups when you have the time, then freeze them for an easy meal when you're busy. Some ingredients are best added to the soup on reheating, such as potatoes and pasta which tend to go mushy when you reheat them. Milk, cream and flour-based thickeners should be added at the reheating stage.

Cream Soups

Another alternative when making soups for the freezer is to cook vegetables in a tasty stock with herbs of your choice, puree and freeze. This takes up less room in the freezer and you have the basis for a cream soup. When you wish to serve the soup, defrost the puree, add more stock if necessary and bring to the boil. Reduce heat, add milk or cream and cook gently until heated through.

Cool Soups

Soups should always be cooled before freezing to avoid bacteria growth. Do this by placing the pot in a sink of cold water. Freeze soup in two to four cup portions so it will freeze faster and thaw faster. Remember you can always use two or three portions if feeding a large number of people. If the number of rigid freezerproof containers is limited, place a freezer bag in a container or bowl and fill the bag with soup, seal and freeze in the container. When frozen, lift out the bag with its contents and store in the freezer – your container is ready to use for something else.

FREEZING POULTRY

Raw Poultry

Purchased poultry requires very little preparation for the freezer, the most important element is choosing the poultry to be frozen, it should be plump, unblemished and odourless. Freeze it as soon as you get home so that it is in peak condition. If the poultry is already in a wrapping, remove from the wrapping and place in a freezer bag or container. To make life easier, prepare the frozen poultry as you wish to use it, before freezing. Chicken for casseroles can be cut into pieces, while breasts for stir-frying can be cubed or cut into strips.

When you are ready to use the frozen poultry, thaw it in the refrigerator. If you wish to marinate it, place it in the marinade so that thawing and marinating can take place simultaneously.

Cooked Poultry

If you intend to freeze cooked poultry dishes, cool quickly in the refrigerator, before packing for freezing. When freezing a large quantity, it is often better to divide the mixture into several portions so that it cools quicker.

Always cook poultry completely before freezing. Never undercook with the idea of finishing the cooking once thawed as this creates the ideal situation for bacteria and the poultry may not heat enough during the remaining cooking time to kill harmful bacteria present. Cooked frozen poultry dishes can be slowly reheated from the frozen state in the oven or on the stovetop if they contain a lot of liquid. If the dish contains little or no liquid it should be thawed in the refrigerator before reheating.

FREEZING MEAT

Raw and cooked meats both store well in the freezer, but as with any food to be frozen, it should be in good condition before freezing. To prepare raw meat for freezing, cut into portions required for a single occasion, such as a family meal. It is easier and more economical to take two packs out of the freezer for extra people than to cook too much through over packing. If the meat is packed when you purchase it remove it from the wrapping and repackage in freezer bags or suitable freezing containers.

THAWING TIMES FOR FROZEN POULTRY	
Type	Defrosting Time in Refrigerator
Whole chickens up to 2 kg (4lb)	12–16 hours
Chickens over 2 kg (4lb)	24–36 hours
Chicken pieces	3–6 hours
Whole turkeys up to 6 kg (12lb)	1–2 days
Turkeys over 6 kg (12lb)	2–3 days
Turkey pieces	3–9 hours
Whole duck up to 2 kg (4lb)	12–16 hours

GLOSSARY OF TERMS

TERM	MEANING
Baste	To moisten meat or vegetables during cooking
Cabbage	Savoy, common garden variety
Capsicum	Sweet red, green or yellow peppers
Cheese, tasty	A firm good-tasting cheddar cheese
Chilli sauce	A sauce which includes chillies, salt and vinegar
Cornflour	Cornstarch, substitute arrowroot
Cream	Light pouring cream
Coconut cream	A thick coconut paste, if unavailable dissolve chopped cream coconut in a little boiling water
Coconut milk	This may be bought in cans in Indian food shops. It is also available in supermarkets as a dried powder which is reconstituted. Or it may be made at home by steeping dessicated coconut in boiling water then pressing in a sieve to extract the liquid
Eggplant	Aubergine
Ghee	Clarified butter which is available from Indian specialty shops. There is also a vegetable fat ghee available
Grill	Broil
Kumera	Orange coloured sweet potato
Lamb shanks	Small knuckle end cuts of leg of lamb
Oyster Sauce	A rich brown bottled sauce made from oysters cooked in salt and soy sauce
Palm sugar	A solid substance made from the syrup of a type of palm tree. If unavailable use soft brown sugar
Puree	Push flesh or cooked food through a sieve or strainer to make a smooth mixture. Alternately you can use the food processor to puree
Snow peas	Mangetout
Sour cream	Commercially soured cream
Shallots	Spring onions
Stock	Homemade gives best results. For convenience, substitute 1 stock cube for every 500 mL (16 fl.oz) water
Sweet potato	Orange-fleshed, known as red potato
Tomato paste	Tomato puree
Vanilla bean	Vanilla pod
Zucchini	Courgette

USEFUL INFORMATION

In this book, ingredients such as fish and meat are given in grams so you know how much to buy.
A small inexpensive set of kitchen scales is always handy and very easy to use. Other ingredients in our recipes
are given in tablespoons and cups, so you will need a nest of measuring cups (1 cup, $^1/_2$ cup, $^1/_3$ cup and $^1/_4$ cup),
a set of spoons (1 tablespoon, 1 teaspoon, $^1/_2$ teaspoon and $^1/_4$ teaspoon) and a transparent graduated
measuring jug (1 litre or 250 mL) for measuring liquids. Cup and spoon measures are level.

MEASURING UP

Metric Measuring Cups

$^1/_4$ cup	60 mL	2 fl.oz
$^1/_3$ cup	80 mL	$2^1/_2$ fl.oz
$^1/_2$ cup	125 mL	4 fl.oz
1 cup	250 mL	8 fl.oz

Metric Measuring Spoons

$^1/_4$ teaspoon	1.25 mL
$^1/_2$ teaspoon	2.5 mL
1 teaspoon	5 mL
1 tablespoon	20 mL

MEASURING DRY INGREDIENTS

Metric	Imperial
15 g	$^1/_2$ oz
30 g	1 oz
60 g	2 oz
90 g	3 oz
125 g	4 oz
155 g	5 oz
185 g	6 oz
220 g	7 oz
250 g	8 oz
280 g	9 oz
315 g	10 oz
350 g	11 oz
375 g	12 oz
410 g	13 oz
440 g	14 oz
470 g	15 oz
500 g	16 oz (1 lb)
750 g	1 lb 8 oz
1 kg	2 lb
1.5 kg	3 lb
2 kg	4 lb
2.5 kg	5 lb

MEASURING LIQUIDS

Metric	Imperial	Cup
30 mL	1 fl.oz	
60 mL	2 fl.oz	$^1/_4$ cup
90 mL	3 fl.oz	
125 mL	4 fl.oz	$^1/_2$ cup
170 mL	$5^1/_2$ fl.oz	$^2/_3$ cup
185 mL	6 fl.oz	
220 mL	7 fl.oz	
250 mL	8 fl.oz	1 cup
500 mL	16 fl.oz	2 cups
600 mL	1 pint	

QUICK CONVERTER

Metric	Imperial
5 mm	$^1/_4$ in
1 cm	$^1/_2$ in
2 cm	$^3/_4$ in
2.5 cm	1 in
5 cm	2 ins
10 cm	4 ins
15 cm	6 ins
20 cm	8 ins
23 cm	9 ins
25 cm	10 ins
30 cm	12 ins

OVEN TEMPERATURES

°C	°F	Gas Mark
120	250	$^1/_2$
140	275	1
150	300	2
160	325	3
180	350	4
190	375	5
200	400	6
220	425	7
240	475	8
250	500	9

QUICK AND EASY PANTRY PLANNING

Try the following tips for no fuss pantry planning.

✦ If you store herbs and spices in alphabetical order, they are easily located and you can quickly see when they need replacing.

✦ Growing a few herbs of your own such as basil, coriander, rosemary, mint, chives and parsley means that you always have these on hand. These fresh herbs are often the secret to delicate flavours in meals.

✦ Place all staples, such as sugar and flour together. Store sauces and condiments according to favourite cuisines, just a glance in the cupboard will give you great ideas.

✦ Keep a good selection of frozen vegetables. Peas, beans, spinach and corn are great standbys and only take minutes to cook in the microwave.

✦ Keep a variety of breads and rolls in the freezer and defrost in the microwave for delicious instant sandwiches.

✦ Cooked pasta and rice freeze well. They reheat in minutes in the microwave and save time on busy nights.

✦ Evaporated milk, available as full cream or skim milk, is a terrific standby when there is no fresh cream. It can be used for sauces and quiches and whips well when chilled. Store a few cans in the pantry for emergencies.

INDEX

ACKNOWLEDGEMENTS

The publishers wish to thank the following
Admiral Appliances; Black & Decker
(Australasia) Pty Ltd; Blanco Appliances;
Knebel Kitchens; Leigh Mardon Pty Ltd;
Master Foods of Australia; Meadow Lea
Foods; Namco Cookware; Ricegrowers'
Co-op Mills Ltd; Sunbeam Corporation
Ltd; Tycraft Pty Ltd distributors of Braun,
Australia; White Wings Foods for their
assistance during recipe testing.

Corso di Fiori; Country Floors; Dansab;
Flossoms; Gallery Nomad; Lifestyle
Imports; Mikassa; Pazotti Tiles; Private
Life; Traditional Elegance; Villa Italiana;
Villeroy and Boch; for their assistance
during photography.

Australian Meat & Livestock Corporation
for their assistance during production.